WRITING IN ICE

Before becoming a writer, Michael Ridpath used to work as a bond trader in the City of London. After writing several financial thrillers, which were published in over 30 languages, he began a crime series featuring the Icelandic detective Magnus Jonson. He has also written five stand-alone thrillers, including *Amnesia, Launch Code* and *The Diplomat's Wife*. He splits his time between London and Massachusetts.

You can find out more about him and his books on his website www.michaelridpath.com or on Facebook.

ALSO BY MICHAEL RIDPATH

WRITING IN ICE

A CRIME WRITER'S GUIDE TO ICELAND

MICHAEL RIDPATH

YARMER

First published in Great Britain in 2021 by Yarmer Head.

Copyright © Michael Ridpath 2021

The moral right of Michael Ridpath to be identified as the author of this work has been asserted by him in accordance with the Copyright, Designs and Patents Act 1988.

Map credit © Jeff Edwards 2021

This is a work of fiction. All the characters in this book are fictitious and any resemblance to actual persons, living or dead, is purely coincidental.

ISBN: 978-1-9997655-6-9

To Pétur Már, Yrsa, Lilja, Ragnar and Quentin
for their generosity and friendship

CONTENTS

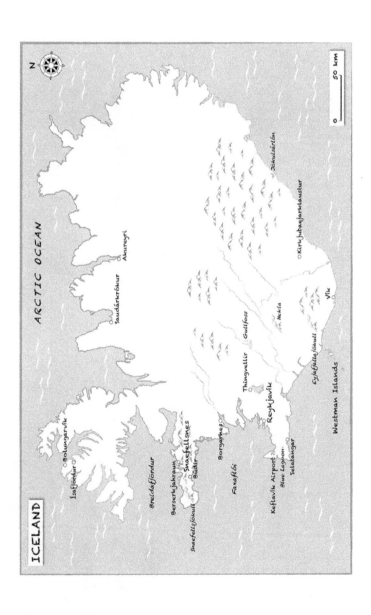

INTRODUCTION

The Icelanders have a saying: '*Glöggt er gests augad*', which means something like 'Clear is a guest's eye'. The idea is that a foreigner can see some things more clearly than a native. I hope it's true; I think it is.

Iceland is an extraordinary country. It is a mixture of the old and the new. This is true of the people: most Icelanders are avid users of social media; most Icelanders' grandmothers have had at least one conversation with an elf. It's also true of the landscape. Very recently, at least in geological terms, Iceland was thrust out of the North Atlantic by the vigorous rubbing together of two tectonic plates, the North American and the European. There are volcanoes active and dormant, lava fields new and old, glaciers made of snow that fell ten thousand years ago, fjords, bleak mountains, green dales. There is wind, rain and snow, and in the interior vast areas of cold desert where there is no precipitation at all. The sun shines sometimes.

It is a country where the extraordinary is ordinary, where at least sometimes it takes a foreigner to point to an everyday Icelandic moment and say: 'Take a look at that!'

In 2007, after a reasonably successful career as an author of financial thrillers, I decided to write a series of detective novels set in Iceland. I knew next to nothing about the country, but it intrigued me.

This is the story of how I set about discovering Iceland, of getting to know the place well enough that I could convincingly set a series of mysteries there. I needed to see the landscape, the capital city, the fishing villages, the farms. But I also needed to meet the people, to understand how they thought, what they liked, what they feared. To get to know them as individuals, not just as Icelanders. To become acquainted with the country's history, its literature, its religion and in particular its folklore.

This is the story of how I fell in love with Iceland.

I hope anyone who has visited Iceland or plans to travel to the country will find something of interest here. I have included small sections on my favourite places in Iceland, a few well known, most less so. This story may also be of interest to anyone with a passing curiosity in how a detective series is put together. Much of the material first appeared on my blog Writing in Ice.

To any Icelanders who pick up this book and feel irritation at my generalizations or impatience with my errors, I say: 'It's your fault for living in such a fascinating country. Get over it.'

With the exception of my publishers and the Icelandic authors, most of the Icelanders in this book are referred to by fictitious names, in order to lightly disguise them. When I first met them, I told them I was researching a novel set in Iceland, so they cannot reasonably have expected to appear in a future book of mine as themselves. Which is why they don't.

A note on accuracy. Much of this book is mostly right;

some of it is slightly wrong. I have been careful not to let a dull fact get in the way of entertaining speculation: see unicorns, hidden people and polar bears in the following pages. Neither is it comprehensive. Many wonderful places to visit in Iceland receive no mention: the towns of Ísafjördur and Akureyri, for example, the waterfalls of Godafoss and Gullfoss, or the geothermal bubblings at Mývatn and Geysir. Yet I do find room for beached whales, lustful berserkers and escaped pufflings.

Now. Let me show you Iceland, and let me introduce you to my detective, Magnus.

1 BOOK TOUR

If you ever fly to Iceland from Europe, be sure to book yourself into a window seat on the right-hand side of the aeroplane. Your first view of Iceland will be unforgettable.

My first landing at Keflavík Airport was in the autumn of 1995. My debut novel, a financial thriller entitled *Free To Trade*, had been published in January that year to an acclaim which was both satisfying and bewildering. I was lucky: it was the right book at the right time for the publishing world, and the following twelve months exploded in the competing demands of a frenzy of publicity and a contractual requirement to sit down and write a second book. I received invitations from foreign publishers to travel to Australia, the United States, France, Norway, Denmark, Holland. And Iceland.

I was urged by my agent to accept most of these invitations, but I didn't really have to go to Iceland. Although its population are avid readers, there are only three hundred thousand of them; it's scarcely an important market in the global scale of things. I knew nothing about the place, but I thought what the hell? It's only three days.

Peering out of the window, the clouds beneath me shredded to reveal the thick finger of black rock that is the Reykjanes Peninsula at the south-west tip of Iceland, pointing towards me. In the distance, bulges of larger, firmer rock, covered in snow, rippled and flexed. A tall plume of smoke, or was it steam, rose upwards from a spot just inland from a small town clinging to the shore.

As the plane descended the rock became rockier, a prairie of stone, gashed and scarred. Browns and yellows and golds emerged from the black, illuminated by an unlikely soft yellow sunshine slinking beneath the clouds prowling out to sea. A single white house sat in a puddle of rich green grass by the shore, where whitecaps nibbled at its boundaries. A windsock stretched out horizontally.

People, there were no trees. Not a one.

The aircraft touched down on a strip of smooth tarmac several miles long miraculously brushed on to this jagged wilderness. We taxied alongside giant camouflaged golf balls, tennis balls, radio masts and radar dishes, passing two enormous US transport planes. We had arrived at one of NATO's most important airbases of the Cold War.

I remembered reading a colleague's country study on Iceland during my days working for an international bank. Mark had pointed out that from the US government's point of view supporting Iceland was cheaper than building an aircraft carrier and it was a lot less likely to sink. From Keflavík, American aircraft could patrol the 'Greenland-Iceland-UK Gap', searching for the Soviet Navy, keeping it out of the North Atlantic seaways to Europe.

At that time, Iceland's international airport took up a small corner of the airbase. I went through passport control and stood by the baggage carousel, where I was met by

Ólafur, my Icelandic publisher. After a warm greeting a thought occurred to me.

'How did you get in here?' I asked. We were, after all, on the air side of the customs barrier.

'No problem,' said Ólafur. 'I'm the consul in Iceland for the Dutch government.'

'That's handy.'

It was the first inkling of something that was going to become increasingly obvious over the following couple of days. Icelanders never have only one job. It is a matter of pride that their nation should have all the trappings of a fully functioning country: diplomats, civil servants, authors, musicians, poets, artists, dancers, footballers. You name it, the Icelanders want to do it. But, with only three hundred thousand people, there are not enough bodies to fill all these posts full time, which is why Ólafur doubled up as Dutch consul. In the coming days I met journalists and publishers who played in the national football league and sang in the national opera.

A year later, Ólafur was the hot favourite in the Reykjavík press for the ultimate Saturday job: president of the country. Sadly, he decided not to run.

Once through customs, we met Pétur, Ólafur's sidekick. Ólafur was the boss: a smooth, sophisticated intellectual in his fifties. Pétur was in his thirties – about my age – tall, blond and austere-looking, with a biting humour delivered in the most Icelandic deadpan. Icelanders have a profound sense of irony, which combines dangerously with a rock-like reserve. You can be speaking to one for several minutes, have decided that they are shy and a little simple, before you realize that they have been gently but effectively taking the piss out of you the whole time without you noticing it. Pétur can still do that to me.

Iceland's international airport is actually forty kilometres outside Reykjavík. The road is a long straight black ribbon pulled taut across a lava field. After a short distance, we turned off on to a rough track and stopped by a series of a dozen or so wooden racks, about eight feet high, on which were dangling what looked like grey-brown rags. These were cod, salted and left out to dry in the wind and occasional sunshine. The resultant stockfish will keep for months, possibly years, and is a delicacy in Portugal and West Africa. Icelanders have been doing this to fish for centuries.

It was a lonely, bleak spot. I looked out over the sea of stone surrounding me. A lonely mountain, in an almost perfect cone, sprouted up a few kilometres away.

'You see all those crevasses?' said Pétur. I looked at the deep gashes on the rolling landscape. 'It's the perfect place to hide a body.'

The thriller writer in me appreciated the point. The soft English desk-worker shivered.

Pétur showed me the frozen lava. It seemed ancient, but was in geological terms brand spanking new. It had been spewed out of a volcano only a few thousand years ago. Then mosses and lichens had grown on it and begun to nibble. They were in brilliant but unlikely colours: bright yellow, lime green, soft orange, glowing brown, a shimmering grey. Eventually the lava crumbles and creates a thin layer of soil to which grasses cling. There were a few clumps of these, already yellow at this time of year.

Later, a little further towards Reykjavík, we passed a fresher lava spew, black as a coal hole, where the lichen was only just beginning to establish itself.

Still no trees.

Next stop was a power station, the source of the plume of steam that I had seen reaching up towards our aeroplane as we landed. The plant took the hot water bubbling out of the earth and converted it to electricity which coursed along power lines to Reykjavík. The process produced hot water, and someone had recently had the bright idea of creating a large swimming pool in the rock to hold the stuff.

October in Iceland is cold: the air was fresh and a stiff breeze bit my cheeks. Ólafur, Pétur and I were wearing coats, but yards away Icelanders were cavorting in the hot water in swimming trunks. The water there is an unreal opaque shade of bright light blue. The Icelanders' skin was a pale pink.

This, of course, was the 'Blue Lagoon', images of which now daub the walls of London Underground stations and bring hordes of tourists flocking to its warmth. I had never heard of it.

We reached Reykjavík. The outskirts of the city reminded me of the outskirts of Warsaw: grey, dull, soulless. Ólafur and Pétur took me to my hotel, which was very comfortable, but housed in an unprepossessing block of grey. I had a shower. Ólafur had told me that almost all Reykjavík's energy came from the magma bubbling beneath the earth, and I could believe it. I emerged from the shower smelling faintly of sulphur.

I had dinner that evening with Ólafur, Pétur and three of their colleagues. On the way, I spotted my first tree! It was squat, no more than ten feet high, its naked, twisted branches shivering in the front garden of a small house. The house itself seemed to be constructed of white-painted corrugated iron with a red-painted iron roof. Indeed, the hill in the centre of Reykjavík seemed to be covered in these brightly painted toy metal houses, gleaming in the evening sunshine. It was all rather jolly.

We went to a crowded restaurant and ate delicious fish. By this time, I was becoming used to dinners with publishers. Publishers are by and large well read, friendly, interesting people. The talk often revolves around books, new and old, and people. Despite the bad press they sometimes get, people in book marketing love books as much as the editors do.

The person in charge of marketing my book was a lively blonde woman named Helga. She asked me whether I had heard of the hidden people.

'No,' I said, puzzled. 'Who are they?' I wondered if they were some specially hard-to-reach target market.

'They are all around us, here in Iceland,' she said.

'OK,' I said, looking around. 'Can I see them?'

'Of course not,' she said. 'They are hidden people. You can't see them.'

'I see,' I said. A lie in so many ways. 'So how do you know they exist?'

Helga went on to explain that some people could in fact see these hidden people at least occasionally, people like her grandmother, who had had a number of dealings with them. They were similar to elves. They lived in rocks all over Iceland, and occasionally imparted their wisdom to the more conventional human inhabitants.

I checked the others around the table. They were listening seriously. I detected a hint of amusement in one of Helga's sales colleagues.

'Do you believe in these hidden people?' I asked Helga.

'Absolutely. Ólafur is an expert on them.'

I checked the sophisticated publisher, who smiled benignly.

'Pétur?' I said. While Helga seemed a little touchy-feely, I thought I could rely on Pétur for some healthy cynicism. 'Do you believe in these elves?'

'Of course I do,' he said, his face granite. I searched for a twinkle, but his blue eyes were dead serious.

I had absolutely no idea. It occurred to me that the entire Icelandic publishing industry might be crazy. Or were they just having me on?

That's the kind of feeling I have often experienced in Iceland.

The conversation shifted, as it often does in Iceland, to the small size of the population and how as a result everyone knows everyone else. Icelanders claim that in a country of only a few hundred thousand people everyone is bound to know everyone else. This is patently not true. The population is similar to the London borough of Barnet, yet most people in Barnet don't know each other. I don't even know most of the people in the block of flats in which I live.

Yet Icelanders do seem to know each other, and if they don't, there will be only one degree of separation: they know someone who knows someone. This is partly because Icelandic extended families are seriously large – a generation back, eight or nine children was not uncommon – which soon leads to dozens of aunts and uncles and cousins. But it's mostly because Icelanders are furious networkers. If they happen to meet a stranger, the first five minutes of conversation is spent triangulating whom they know in common.

There really were very few famous Icelanders in the 1990s. In fact there was just one: the singer, Björk. Ólafur was pointing out how even the most famous Icelanders were down to earth, how a postman would address the president by her first name – the president was a woman at that time

– and how you might come across a celebrity acting like a normal person in a bar.

'Like Björk,' said Helga. 'Have you heard of Björk, the singer?'

'Of course,' I said.

'Well, she is sitting just over there. Right behind you.'

I wasn't going to be made a fool of twice in one evening. I glanced at Pétur, who almost smiled, and I refused to turn around.

But when we left the restaurant, I glanced back at the noisy group in the corner behind me, in the middle of which was a small woman with short black hair and very pale high cheekbones, laughing.

Björk.

A couple of years later, I went on a book tour to Germany. It was here I learned that despite British rumours to the contrary, Germans do actually have a sense of humour. At any rate, they laughed at me several times, and they were set off into hysterics by a small Swedish lady named Maj Sjöwall, who read to them something about the police surrounding a dog. I was leaving the event when one of my fellow authors, a German crime novelist, mentioned she had once visited Iceland.

'So have I,' I said. 'It's a seriously weird country.'

'But wouldn't it be a great place to set a novel?'

'Absolutely.'

'Why don't you write one?' she asked.

'I write financial thrillers,' I said. 'I don't see how I could possibly write one of those set in Iceland. The country is too small; their banks are tiny. I doubt there is any financial crime there.'

'That's a shame.'

'Yes,' I said. 'It is.'

And I thought no more about the country for ten years.

2 THE PROBLEM

In the autumn of 2007 I had a problem. I hoped – I prayed – that Iceland was the solution.

Every successful author has a moment of good fortune. For me, it was right at the very beginning of my career. In 1993 Carole Blake, the 'Blake' of the Blake Friedmann Literary Agency, fell while on holiday in the South of France and broke her leg.

I was working in the City at the time, as a bond trader. I had decided to write a novel. On the strength of the excellent advice to write what you know, I wrote a thriller about a bond trader. It was called *Free To Trade*. After years of writing and rewriting, I bought a pretty box with flowers on it from the department store John Lewis, printed off the manuscript, put the manuscript into the box and sent it off to agents. Actually, I initially sent them the first two chapters plus the synopsis.

All agents and publishers have a 'slush pile'. Nowadays, it is a virtual pile of zeroes and noughts stored in servers around the world; then, it was an actual pile several feet high of manuscripts sent in from would-be authors. Since Carole had broken her leg, she decided to go through her slush pile with more care than she could usually give it, and she found *Free To Trade*.

Little did I know, but my timing was perfect.

In 1993 the world was coming out of an unpleasant recession and the Cold War had finished. Publishers had retrenched, sticking to tried-and-trusted authors like Frederick Forsyth, John le Carré and Dick Francis. But then John Grisham's *The Firm* was published, a legal thriller written by a youngish American author, and things changed. White-collar crime was the successor to the spy thriller. The hunt was on for 'the British John Grisham'. And then *Free To Trade* popped up.

Carole was no slouch. She applied her considerable enthusiasm to securing me publishers in Britain, America and over thirty other countries, including Iceland. Despite my publishers proclaiming otherwise, I never was 'the British John Grisham', but *Free To Trade* was successful when it was published in 1995, reaching number two in the British bestseller lists, and staying in the top ten for three months.

Over the next ten years, I wrote seven more financial thrillers. The first three or four reached the top ten, but sales slowly, inexorably, declined. There were a number of possible reasons for this: people preferred to read about courtrooms than about trading rooms, legal thrillers themselves were beginning to decline in popularity, there was a screw-up at my publishers' warehouse which meant bookshops couldn't get my books. But during those ten years, I was learning my craft and my writing was improving.

I was a big fish in a tiny pool, the puddle that was financial thrillers, and I began to wonder how I would measure up against the Frederick Forsyths and John le Carrés at their own game. So, when my publisher decided to drop my books, I decided to try my hand at a spy thriller.

I settled on Berlin in 1938 and spent two years researching, plotting and writing a novel involving a young German and a young Briton who were friends and who wanted to overthrow Hitler. Carole read it and suggested some rewriting: there was too much research and not enough pace. After the rewriting, it was too predictable and lacked texture. Eventually, we arrived at something we were both happy with and we sent it out to twelve publishers.

Who declined it. All of them.

Now I was in trouble. Advances continue to roll in from individual books for a couple of years after you have written them, so I had had a breathing space to write my spy thriller, but now the income was drying up fast.

Plan B had failed. I needed a Plan C. I needed it quickly and it had to work.

This time, I wanted to make sure that whatever book I wrote, someone would publish it. And they would publish it, because it would sell. I needed to write a book that might end up on the shelves of a small branch of Smith's.

So I checked out my local WHSmith's in Temple Fortune in North London. I was looking for six-inch sections of bookshelves given over to individual authors of the type I could aspire to be. Aside from the old traditional favourites – the Frederick Forsyths and the Dick Francises – there seemed to be two distinct categories of novel that I might possibly write: Dan Brown-type stories featuring an international conspiracy, or crime novels featuring distinctive detectives. I've never been one for conspiracy theories, so I needed to get myself a distinctive detective.

Crime fiction is perennially popular, but that means there are hundreds of detectives out there. How could mine be different? One approach would be to give him (or her) a distinctive job, or a disability, mental or physical, or to place him in an interesting part of Britain. But I had written eight novels set all over the world. I didn't want to confine myself to my own place of birth. I needed a distinctive country.

At that moment, Iceland popped into my head. I should have just stopped then, gone home and started researching, but I am an analytical type, sometimes *too* analytical. I went home and started thinking, scribbling in notebooks, umming and ahhing. Eventually I came up with an idea involving a policeman in Saudi Arabia. It was quite a clever idea: I won't tell you too much about it because I might yet use it. I was tempted.

But this idea, whatever it was, had to work. Fortunately, I decided to try the idea out on friends and acquaintances. 'Which would you rather buy, a book featuring an Icelandic detective, or a Saudi detective?'

Almost everyone preferred Iceland. They didn't know much about the country, but they thought it was intriguing and they would like to find out more. Saudi Arabia, not so much.

So, Iceland it was.

Next, I needed a detective, and I needed a plot. More on the detective later. The plot for my first book in the series needed to be distinctive too.

Most plots of crime novels, and most crime in real life, involve families, local communities, people who know and live close to each other. My financial thrillers had been international in nature, involving people from many different nationalities and often taking place in several different countries in one book. My first case needed to take place in Iceland. But I liked the idea of an international backdrop, something with a global impact.

Stumped.

I remember exactly where I was when I solved this particular problem. My daughter and I were on a 'College Tour' of US universities that she was considering applying to, and I was sitting on a bench outside a classroom at Tufts University in Boston as she listened in to a class.

I remembered that local branch of WHSmith's and that other category of books taking up shelf space. Dan Brown. *The Da Vinci Code* had been published four years before with great success: it was the story of how certain facts about Jesus had been hidden for centuries. Was there a story or myth with as global a reach as Christianity that might involve Iceland?

What a stupid question.

But it was a stupid question with an answer. *The Lord of the Rings*.

OK, *The Lord of the Rings* doesn't quite have the global impact of Christianity. But it is a story that is known throughout the world. The book was voted the most popular published in the twentieth century by British readers. The films of the book had been seen by tens of millions of people around the world. And Middle Earth sounded a lot like Iceland.

What if Tolkien had been inspired by an Icelandic saga? He probably *had* been inspired by an Icelandic saga. So what if he had been inspired by a lost Icelandic saga that someone had found? And that someone had been murdered. And my detective had to sort it out.

I liked the idea. I *loved* the idea. And at this stage, the very beginning of the process of writing a novel, the most important thing is that the author loves the idea. Readers come later.

Now all I had to do was find out about Iceland.

3 HISTORY

I began to read. At this stage I was just trying to get a general idea of the country, its society and its people. Wide was good; serendipity ruled. I had done this before: I had set books in Brazil and South Africa, and Iceland is much smaller than those two countries, and therefore less daunting.

The first book I picked up was *Dreaming of Iceland* by Sally Magnusson, a charming description of a one-week holiday the author took with her famous father Magnus back to his homeland. Then I read *Ring of Seasons*, by Terry Lacy, an American who has lived in Iceland for many years, and *The Killer's Guide to Iceland* by Zane Radcliffe, an excellent novel about an Englishman visiting the country and getting himself into deep trouble. Radcliffe has a way with food similes: lava like digestive biscuits, glaciers like icing on a cake. It sounds corny, but it's actually rather good.

I assumed that there were no crime writers of note in Iceland, which was unforgivably naive. In fact, Arnaldur Indridason had written several novels translated into English, one of which, *Silence of the Grave,* had won the

British Crime Writers' Association Gold Dagger in 2005. Crime writers like to claim that their novels shine a powerful light on the societies in which they are set, and I think they are correct. Arnaldur and his detective Erlendur introduced me to a useful range of fictional Icelanders.

On a more mundane level, the 'Contexts' sections of the Lonely Planet and Rough Guides were excellent. I find the authors of these guides in particular are diligent and careful and their books are packed full of useful detail.

W. H. Auden and his friend Louis MacNeice produced a whimsical collection of poems and diary entries as payment to Faber for a holiday in Iceland in the 1930s, when the country was the poorest in Europe. This was updated imaginatively by the modern British poets Simon Armitage and Glyn Maxwell, chronicling their own Icelandic travels in *Moon Country*.

I soon encountered the *Iceland Review*, a quarterly magazine with stunning photographs and interesting articles about all aspects of Icelandic life. The magazine is online, of course, but it's better in its physical version. The *Iceland Weather Report* was a blog by the Icelandic-Canadian Alda Sigmundsdóttir. The blog no longer exists, but Alda is well worth following on Facebook and elsewhere: over the years, she has given me all sorts of information and ideas. *The Reykjavík Grapevine* is an excellent weekly English-language newspaper with a good web presence.

I bought DVDs; I wanted to see what the country actually looked like. *101 Reykjavík*, a film of the book by Hallgrímur Helgason, is an enjoyable story of Reykjavík's nightlife. *Nói Albinói* is a bleak tale of the bleak life of a bleak teenager in a small, isolated town in the middle of winter. *The Seagull's Laughter* is a sweet film set in a fishing village in Iceland in the 1950s.

I was beginning to get some idea of what Iceland was like. For a much fuller description of my sources of information on the country, including those published in the last ten years, see the Appendix.

I studied history at university, and I like to know the history of any country I write about. Given my intended plot for the first book in the series, this was especially necessary. There are, of course, many histories of Iceland, but the one I stumbled across first was *Iceland Saga* by Magnus Magnusson. This is more than a history. Magnusson takes his reader on a journey around Iceland to the locations where the major events in the country's early history took place. The book really fired my imagination.

Before there were people in Iceland, there were trees. Really. In the ninth century the whole country was covered with trees, and there wasn't a soul to cut them down.

There are hints that Irish monks may have inhabited Iceland during the early ninth century, and a couple of wayward Viking sailors stumbled across the island while lost, but the first Viking that we know of who sailed there deliberately was a man called Flóki. He took three ravens with him to help him find Iceland. He let them loose. The first two returned to the ship, but the third flew straight off over the horizon. Flóki followed it and made landfall.

At first Flóki was dismayed by the cold. He climbed to the top of a mountain and looking out at drift ice choking the island's fjords, so he decided to call the country 'Iceland'. He returned to Norway disappointed, although one of his mates claimed that in spring butter dripped from every blade of grass. This optimist was henceforth known as 'Butter' Thórólfur, in perhaps the first recorded example of Icelandic irony.

The first visitor to Iceland who actually stayed was Ingólfur Arnarson. He set out from Norway in 874, and when he spied the mountains of Iceland, he threw his high seat pillars into the sea, vowing to make his home wherever they fetched up. I've never been able to figure out precisely what these 'high seat pillars' were: presumably pieces of a disassembled chair. This does, at least, sound authentically Scandinavian.

Although he made landfall right away, at a place coincidentally called Ingólfshöfdi, or Ingólfur's Cape, it took him many months to find his chair. Eventually two of his slaves discovered it in a smoky bay on the west coast, the smoke coming from hot springs. So this was where Ingólfur made his home. He decided to call the smoky bay 'Smoky Bay' or Reykjavík. You will see throughout this book that the settlers were not very imaginative in their choice of place names.

Norway was becoming crowded, and a lot of people didn't like their king Harald Fair-Hair (or 'Fine-Hair' depending on your view of Viking hairdressing, 'fine' as in 'beautiful' rather than 'thin'), so a number sailed off to Iceland in search of free land. They brought their sheep and horses with them, and cut down the trees for firewood. Since sheep nibble tree saplings, and the soil in Iceland is particularly thin, the trees never managed to re-establish themselves. Forestry wasn't helped by the tendency of volcanoes to dump molten lava over the landscape at irregular intervals. Now there are so few trees you can go a whole day without seeing one.

The couple of hundred years after Ingólfur's arrival are

known as the Settlement Period. To my mind, the most extraordinary thing about this time was that there was no ruler. No king, no emperor, no prince, not even a prime minister. This was a relatively warm period of European history, and so it was possible to grow crops and feed livestock successfully. The outer rim of the island was dotted with farms. Farmers would gather at a local meeting place, known as a *thing*. Once a year, their leaders, or *godar* as they were known, would travel to the general assembly, or 'Althing', at Thingvellir in the south-west of the country near Reykjavík.

Thingvellir was, and still is, an extraordinary place. It is set in a narrow gorge where the two continental plates meet, next to a flat valley floor. (This is Iceland, gorges can be *next to* valley floors, not above or below them; the land moves around a lot.) At the start of the proceedings the Law Speaker would stand on the Law Speaker's Rock and recite a third of the laws from memory for three whole days. It took him three years to get through the lot. This was before they knew how to write laws down. The *godar* would then settle their disputes according to these laws, judged by their peers. There were occasional flashes of violence, but usually disputes were resolved peacefully. Outlawry was a punishment for serious crimes, where the guilty party would be sent either into the desolate interior of the country or abroad for a number of years.

The system worked for several hundred years, until it all fell apart at the end of the thirteenth century. It is all described in the 'sagas', or 'stories', which were originally oral tales, not written down until the thirteenth century. More on them later.

During this time, Iceland was mostly peaceful. There were occasional skirmishes between farmers, but never full-scale battles. However, it would be wrong to characterize the Icelanders as peace-loving farmers: these were Vikings after all.

Some historians can become quite grumpy about the term 'Vikings' and the suggestion that they were nothing more than a bunch of bloodthirsty rapists. They see the early Icelanders as traders and artists, not looters and pillagers. The term 'Viking' comes from the word *vík*, which as we have seen means 'bay'; it can also mean port or trading post, as in Norwich in England. So the Vikings were what Norsemen were called when they went travelling; the sagas are full of young men who spend a gap year 'raiding and trading' before returning to their farms in Iceland. These historians also complain that Vikings get a bad rep from the people they were raping and pillaging: monks in Britain, Ireland, France, the Netherlands, Germany, Russia and Sicily, who had an unfair propaganda advantage over their adversaries in that they knew how to write down what happened. Well, those that survived could. Actually, the Norsemen were capable of great art and poetry (true) and liked to cuddle lambs (also true).

As in all good crime stories, forensics settle the dispute, in this case DNA evidence. A recent study of the Icelanders' genome shows that while 75 per cent of the patrilineal DNA comes from Scandinavia, less than 40 per cent of the matrilineal DNA came from there – 62 per cent came from Ireland and Scotland. So in the past, the majority of men were Norwegians and the majority of women came from the British Isles. My reading of this is many of the raiders and traders came home with women from their years abroad. Slave women.

Christianity came to Iceland in the year 1000. Olaf Tryggvason, the King of Norway, had converted a few years earlier and was eager to spread the word across the Viking world. This was decided, of course, at the Althing. After days of speeches and acrimony, at which it looked for a moment as if the country would split into two groups with two different sets of laws – pagans and Christians – the decision was given to the Law Speaker of many years, the pagan but very wise Thorgeir.

Thorgeir lay down in his booth, put a fur cloak over his head and had a good long think. It lasted all day and all night. In the morning, he emerged and announced that henceforward Icelanders would be Christians. There then arose a problem: a lot of people needed to be baptized in a hurry. There was a river handy at Thingvellir, the powerful, fast-flowing Öxará, but – in one of the most un-Icelandic moments in Iceland's history – the chieftains decided that that river was a bit cold, and rode off to the geothermally warm waters of Laugarvatn a few miles away to be dunked.

With Christianity came writing and reading, pastimes that Icelanders have taken to with alacrity over the centuries. It is likely that literacy was higher in Iceland than in the other medieval countries of Europe. The reason is probably the nature of settlements in Iceland. The countryside is dotted with individual farms, rather than the more common villages of Europe. While some of the larger of these farms had their own churches, most did not. This meant that Icelanders had to do their own reading of the Bible; they couldn't rely on priests to do it for them. This literacy was no doubt a reason for the sophistication of the sagas, the beauty of the medieval poetry and the determination of every Icelander since then to write a book.

From Iceland, adventurous Norsemen ventured further afield. Erik the Red, an outlaw, sailed from Iceland in 982 to Greenland, and built himself a farm there. Amazingly, the south-west corner of Greenland is indeed green, as we will see in a later chapter. From Eriksfjord, Erik's son and daughter-in-law took a band of followers south and west to what they called Vinland, but what we now call North America. It is tantalizingly unclear exactly where they stopped for a couple of summers, although a Viking settlement was discovered in Newfoundland in 1961.

The system of government around the Althing lasted until the late thirteenth century, when there was a series of armed clashes between the *godar*, ending with an appeal to the King of Norway to take charge in 1264. This he did. Which turned out to be not such a good idea in the long term. The plan was for the Althing to maintain its authority, but over time the power of the Norwegian king in Iceland's affairs grew. Then, in a bewildering session of a medieval version of the board game *Risk*, Norway and Sweden united with Denmark. The Danes ended up being in charge, and over the following centuries they established a monopoly of trade with Iceland. Iceland became a very poor country, one of the poorest in Europe.

At this time also, Europe was in the throes of the mini-ice age. The climate was becoming colder, which can't have helped Icelandic farmers much. They could no longer grow barley. The Greenland settlement died out, its ports frozen, its crops failing, and the local Inuit outcompeting the Norsemen for game. Trade with the rest of Europe was constrained by increasing interference from the Danish government. There were no towns, and villages were small. People lived in hovels of rock, and earth, with turf roofs. Every year, farmers feared not having enough hay to see them through the winter, as they huddled in a single room above their livestock, surrounded by darkness and snow. Spring was the time of starvation, when the crops were planted, the grass was beginning to grow, but as yet there was nothing to feed the sheep or the family cow. There was a feudal system of sorts: rich farmers and poor peasants, but in truth the rich farmers were poor.

And the Icelanders were farmers. The sea around Iceland was teeming with cod and herring, but this was fished by large ships from England, France and Germany. There was some illicit trade with these foreigners, but not much. Foreigners came from further afield than Western Europe. Barbary pirates found Icelandic women easy pickings, plucking them from defenceless coastal communities and whisking them back to the bazaars of North Africa.

There was, however, one secret source of wealth for the Icelanders during the Middle Ages. Unicorn horn.

Unicorns were much prized in Europe: unicorn horn was the most prestigious material to display at court, and ground up it had potent medicinal strength. The fact that unicorns don't actually exist wasn't an insuperable problem for Icelanders and Danish merchants. The narwhal is a small whale with a long spiral horn which is found in the waters around Greenland. Narwhal horn was imported into western Iceland and unicorn horn was exported from eastern Iceland to Denmark, whence it was sold all over Europe.

Iceland reached its nadir at the time of the eruption of the volcano Laki in 1783. This was one of those eruptions, similar to but bigger than Eyjafjallajökull in 2010, which threw tons of ash and in particular sulphur dioxide into the atmosphere. The resulting 'Haze Famine' led to the deaths of 80 per cent of the sheep and a quarter of the population. At one point, the remaining Icelanders considered abandoning their country entirely, leaving it to the volcanoes, the glaciers and the bitter cold (see Chapter Fifteen).

In the following century Icelanders legged it to North America in large numbers, setting up communities in the Midwest and Canada, such as the town of Gimli in Manitoba. These Vestur-Íslendingar would sometimes return home with fancy clothes and stories of wooden houses and roofs which didn't leak.

Families were large, and then they weren't, as children died young.

Wealthier Icelanders went abroad for education, to Denmark. They returned to their homeland with ideas. Ideas about national identity, ideas about independence. The Danes gradually acceded to Icelanders' demands. Independence came in stages: Iceland got its own constitution in 1874; in 1918 Iceland was recognized as a sovereign state under the Danish Crown; and finally, in 1944, while Denmark was under Nazi occupation, Iceland declared itself a republic.

The relationship between Denmark and Iceland is a tricky one. On the one hand, Denmark is and has been for many years a remarkably civilized society with progressive values. Most educated Icelanders used to receive their postgraduate university education there, and many still do. Until quite recently, Danish was the foreign language taught first in schools. And yet. I have met Danes who have been eager to explain Iceland to me on the basis that the country was a former colony of theirs, in the same way a Briton might have spoken about India in the 1960s. While some Icelanders idolize anything Danish, others are suspicious of their former colonial masters. If Danes try to speak to them in Danish, an Icelander will reply in English.

The First World War, sometimes dubbed the 'Good

War' by contemporary writers, was a boom time for Icelanders, as Britain in particular became desperate to import food. But then the Depression took its toll, and in the Second World War the country was invaded. On 9 May 1940, Hitler unleashed his cunning master plan to invade Belgium, Luxembourg and Holland, to outflank the French and British armies and within weeks to overrun France itself. On that very same day, the British unleashed their own master plan, to invade Iceland, over a thousand miles in the wrong direction from Belgium.

The British invasion was a total success. They landed, put up their tents and made tea. The Icelanders were a little miffed, but decided to be polite and treat the occupying army as guests. At one point, there were 25,000 British servicemen in Iceland. They provided jobs and wages for the inhabitants. Things really looked up in July 1941, when the British handed over the occupation of the island to 40,000 Americans. The Americans paid higher wages, and brought chewing gum and nylon stockings to the island. There were at that point more young American men than young Icelandic males in the country. Some say it was a good time to be a young Icelandic woman.

This was when Iceland's fortunes really turned around. The country moved rapidly from being the poorest country in Europe on a per capita basis in the 1940s to becoming the richest in 2007. Some of this wealth came directly from the US base, which was expanded during the Cold War. Some of it came from the fish, which the Icelanders now caught for themselves. And some of it came from a highly educated, hard-working population creating wealth. Icelanders fought three 'cod wars' against the British in the 1950s through to the 1970s, establishing their right to extend their fishing limits from three miles, to four miles, to fifty miles and then to two hundred miles. Iceland's fishing villages boomed; England's fishing port of Hull went bust.

All countries are a product of their history. You have to be tough to have survived Iceland's past: the cold, the long, isolated winters of hunger, the long summers of back-breaking toil. It's worth remembering this. The twenty-first-century Icelander in his Ray-Bans, driving his BMW 4 × 4 home to his geothermally heated minimalist apartment in Reykjavík is only a generation or two away from almost unimaginable hardship. Dump him on a snowy mountain in the dark miles from anywhere and he will probably know what to do. Put him behind the wheel of his BMW, and he might get a little over-excited; it's probably a good idea to be extra careful when crossing the road in Reykjavík.

FAVOURITE PLACES – THINGVELLIR

Thingvellir, or 'Parliament Fields', is one of those rare places in the world: it is steeped in history, it is geologically extraordinary and its beauty takes your breath away.

It is about forty kilometres to the east of Reykjavík. Once you escape the city's suburbs you turn inland and drive through dramatic, desolate mountains. You descend to the entrance of what is now a national park and, after a kilometre or so, stop your car at the floor of a green valley. To the east rise rough foothills, to the west a dramatic cliff face of grizzled grey rock. A clear stream runs through the valley past a church to a sizeable lake, Thingvallavatn.

Small wooden bridges span the river. Stop on one of these and stare down at the stream into deep pools of clear water whose colour changes and shifts depending on the sky, the clouds and the angle of the sun. A host of native Icelandic plants line the pools: birch, willow, crowberries, bilberries, heathers, tiny flowers and all kinds of mosses and lichens. In autumn, these pools reflect red, yellow, orange, gold and russet, and become the subjects of some of the most stunning photographs in Iceland.

You take a footpath up to the cliff from the valley floor. It turns out that the cliff is actually two cliffs, with a narrow gorge, known as the Almannagjá, running between them for five miles parallel to the valley below. This is part of the long rift that runs diagonally from the north-east of Iceland to the south-west, separating Europe from North America, a rift that incites volcanoes, earthquakes, and the mysterious depths of Lake Thingvellir, where scuba divers explore the scar between continents underwater. A river, the Öxará, tumbles over the top of the cliff and along the gorge in a couple of powerful waterfalls, before falling down to the valley. As the North American and European continents grind up against each other, the valley moves; geologists estimate that it has widened by about eight metres and subsided by four metres since the country was settled a thousand years ago.

And now comes the history. At the top of these cliffs, the Law Speaker's Rock juts out, from where the Law Speaker could look out over the *godar* and their companions assembled in the valley below him. You can still see the rock and the ruins of stone booths where the *godar* stayed during the Althing. Here the intricate legal stratagems devised by Njal in *Njal's Saga* were acted out. And in the tumult of the Öxarárfoss, witches were drowned.

This place has a claim to be the site of the oldest parliament in the world. But rather than being housed in a magnificent building, it is located outside in a valley of desolation and beauty. Standing in the Westminster Hall of the Houses of Parliament in London, you feel a sense of awe in the womb of the 'mother of parliaments'. The sense of awe you feel when standing by the Law Speaker's Rock at Thingvellir is in some ways very similar, and in some ways so very different.

In 1944 Thingvellir was crowded with Icelanders celebrating independence. It was filled again in 1974 when they were celebrating the centenary of their constitution. It can get crowded, too, in July and August, this time with tour buses. For Thingvellir is one of the three stops on the tourists' 'Golden Circle', the others being Gullfoss and Geysir. Last time I visited was on a damp Friday morning in November, and it was nearly empty. And very beautiful.

4 LANGUAGE

I have tried hard to learn Icelandic, I really have. For two stints of several months each, I spent three-quarters of an hour every morning listening to audio files and reading grammar and teach-yourself books. At first it seemed easy. Many words, especially the simpler ones, are close to English. For example, *sokkur* is 'sock', *takk* is 'thanks' and *blár* is 'blue'. Easy, right?

Wrong. The grammar is a killer. Everything has to agree with everything else. There are cases, moods, tenses, genders. It's like Latin, but more complicated. And the natives really care if you get it right. For example, the words for the first four numbers are significantly different depending on the gender of the thing you are counting. In French you only need five words to count to four: *un, une, deux, trois, quatre*. In Icelandic you need twelve: *einn, ein, eitt, tveir, tvaer, tvö, thrír, thrjár, thrjú, fjórir, fjórar, fjögur*. I mean, really. And should you ever need to say 'the four blue tables', you need to make 'four' and 'blue' agree with tables. And you need to use the correct form of 'the' and stick it on the end of the table. If you do ever find yourself in a restaurant, one with multicoloured furniture, and have a desire to say 'the four blue tables', my advice is hold up four fingers and point.

Or just say it in English. They all speak English.

You see, in one important way, Icelandic is about the most futile language to study. Not only are there only three hundred thousand speakers (compared to over a billion Mandarin Chinese speakers, for example) but almost all of them speak English. On my first visit to Iceland, when I proudly tried my *góðan dag* – 'good day' – in shops, nearly everyone replied in English. And after a couple of days, I realized that the ones who did answer in Icelandic were Poles, who hadn't cottoned on that I was a foreigner.

Just about everyone under the age of sixty speaks English, and often extremely good English. So do most of those older than that. This situation, when everyone speaks another more widespread language, is known as 'diglossia', and linguistic theory suggests that the less widespread language will die out.

I am not so sure. Everyone is proud of their language, but Icelanders are *really* proud of theirs. In a country with no ancient architecture, but with a rich literary history, language is important. Bilingual Icelanders write massive amounts of poetry and prose in Icelandic. They have spelling wars: there was an epic struggle in the Great Spelling War of 1941, followed by a rematch in the Second Spelling War of 1974, with the Nobel Laureate Halldór Laxness taking on the Icelandic literary establishment in a fight to make spelling more phonetic. Rock bands, such as Sigur Rós, sing in Icelandic (of a sort) rather than English. Icelanders are infuriatingly pedantic when it comes to their medieval grammar; the Icelandic language is not something they will let go of lightly.

But there is a point to learning a little Icelandic. It's fascinating.

Icelandic is a lightly modified version of Old Norse, the language of the sagas, and of those Viking tourists I described in the last chapter. Hence the complicated grammar. Its relationship to Danish, Swedish or Norwegian is similar to that of Latin to Italian or Spanish: possible to make out individual words, difficult to understand complete sentences rapidly spoken. Norwegian and Danish are much simpler.

The pronunciation is phonetic and mostly follows consistent rules. They roll their 'r's wonderfully, and the 'g's disappear somewhere in the back of their throat. There are some weirdnesses, for example 'Keflavík' becomes 'Keplavik'. The word for yes, *já*, pronounced 'yow', is often sucked rather than spoken. It's just about possible to speak and understand individual words and short sentences; after years of practice I can now say the name of the volcano Eyjafjallajökull. Auden has a useful tip. He wrote: 'We are going around a thing called the Langjökull [a glacier]; if you want to pronounce it you must move your mouth both ways at once, draw your tongue through your uvula and pray to St David of Wales.'

Icelandic has two great little letters. *Thorn* is like a p with the line on the left sticking up higher, and is pronounced like the 'th' in 'thing'. *Eth* is like a d, with a curved line, and is pronounced like the 'th' in 'this'. Both letters come from Old English, and were introduced by the monks from Britain who first tried to write in Icelandic. Unlike Old English and the monks, *thorn* and *eth* have survived.

Writing these in English is tricky. These days digital technology means you can now type the Icelandic letters themselves, but it's counterintuitive for English speakers: the god Thór becomes something that looks a lot like Þór, which seems much less mighty. The convention often used, and which I have used here, is to write 'th' for *thorn* and 'd' for *eth*. The major difficulty with this is that half the time 'd' is therefore pronounced 'th', for example the word *bord*, meaning table, is pronounced 'borthe'. Quentin Bates, the English writer of Icelandic crime novels, is so irritated by this that he bans any characters from his books whose names include this letter: no Davíds, no Sigurdurs, no Gudrúns. I think if I had my druthers, I would write the letter 'eth' as 'dd' like the 'th' sound in the Welsh county of Gwynedd. That would make it 'drudders'. Hmm.

There are no 'c's, 'w's or 'z's in Icelandic, but they do have one other letter, 'æ', which is an 'a' and an 'e' squished together, and sounds like 'eye'. Accents are very important: vowels with accents are entirely different letters, with their own place in the alphabet. They are also pronounced differently, so 'a' is long as in 'father' and 'á' is painful as in 'now'. Never leave them out because it will make Icelanders grumpy. I have intentionally left a couple out in this book to prove my point.

Which brings us to names. The Icelanders have a unique approach to naming people. It ranges from the simple, Jón Jónsson, a boy's name, to the more complicated Boghildur Dögg Skarphédinsdottir, a snappy girl's name. The system works as follows.

Your 'last name' is your father's name, plus '–son' if you are a boy, or '–dóttir' if you are a girl. There is no surname in a conventional European or American sense. So I would be Michael Andrewsson, since my father's name was Andrew. My sister would be Mary Andrewsdóttir. My grandfathers' names were Claude and Conrad, so my parents would be Andrew Claudesson and Elizabeth Conradsdóttir. This seems noble is some ways: our parents are honoured and my sister and mother have names which respect their sex – there is something fundamentally illogical about the English name Jane Johnson, for example. But our tight little family of four all end up with different last names, which can be a little weird when we try to check into a hotel together.

Of course, all rules are made to be broken. During the nineteenth century, some Icelanders affected Danish-style surnames, often having returned from university there. Thus there are a few Icelanders who go by the traditional European naming system – Élin Briem, for example. Other examples of surnames are Blöndal, Thorlacius, Hansen, Nordal and Möller. This practice was banned as un-Icelandic in the twentieth century, but those who already had Danish-style last names were allowed to keep them.

Diminutives are often used: Gunni, for Gunnar, Magga for Margrét. There are thirty-five confusing boys' names and thirty-three girls' names beginning 'Sigur–' . Fortunately, the boys are all called Siggi and the girls Sigga.

In times past, the Vikings were more imaginative with their nicknames. The sagas include Audun the Stutterer, Eystein Foul-Fart, Ulf the Squint-Eyed, Thorberg Ship-Breast and Ljótur the Unwashed. My favourite is the name of one of the most influential of the original settlers in Iceland, Aud the Deep-Minded, daughter of Ketil Flat-Nose.

In more modern times, as the number of Icelanders has proliferated, it has become more important to tell the Jón Jónssons apart. Hence the increasing use of middle names, many of which are one syllable, such as Örn, Thór or Dögg.

You may have wondered how I knew there were exactly

thirty-five boys' names beginning with 'Sigur'. You did, didn't you? Well, there is an official book of names, which I have open in front of me. You cannot give your child a name unless it is on the list. Every year a committee adds to the names. The book is stuffed full of wonderful Nordic creations such as Gunnthóra, Dagbjört and Ragnheidur, but there are also the more conventional biblical Davíd, Símon and Sara, as well as the modern-sounding Karlotta and Marvin. Somehow Michael crept in there, along with Carl, Cecil and Christian, even though the letter 'c' doesn't really exist in Icelandic. Disappointing.

The Icelandic last name, a patronymic, is subtly different from the European surname. Gunnar Jónsson is the Gunnar whose father is Jón, whereas Michael Ridpath means that I am part of the Ridpath family as well as being called Michael. More practically, there are many more Michaels than Ridpaths. So, in more formal situations, or in official lists or phone books, for example, I would be known as 'Mr Ridpath', or show up as 'Ridpath, M.' This doesn't apply in Iceland. 'Jónsson' is more or less as common as 'Gunnar'. And Gunnar is more Gunnar than Jónsson. So Gunnar is called Gunnar in most situations, however formal, even if he becomes president, and he will be listed as Gunnar in the national phone book.

This has its advantages. Two of the top Icelandic crime writers are Yrsa Sigurdardóttir (she has dark hair) and Lilja Sigurdardóttir (she has blonde hair). They are not sisters, but both their fathers happened to be called Sigurdur, a common name. It is much easier and clearer to speak about books by Yrsa and Lilja, than by Sigurdardóttir and Sigurdardóttir.

This naming system posed problems for my detective Magnus, whom we will meet properly in the next chapter.

His father was Ragnar, and his grandfather was Jón. So in Iceland, Magnus was Magnús Ragnarsson, and his father was Ragnar Jónsson. When Magnus came to the United States to be with his father, this caused difficulties for the American bureaucracy, and so he took his father's last name and anglicized it slightly to Jonson. Of course, when he returned to Iceland, he retook his father's first name as his last name. So Magnus Jonson became Magnús Ragnarsson, a constant reminder of his confused identity. By the way, I show this by employing the American 'Magnus' in prose or when characters are speaking in English, but 'Magnús' when they are speaking in Icelandic. It drives my copy editors mad.

Now, if you think the term 'pedant' is a badge of honour or a term of endearment read on. If you prefer to use it as an insult to hurl at annoying nit-pickers, skip the next couple of paragraphs. I know from uncomfortable experience that a distressing number of my readers are proud of their pedantry.

Translating place names can be tricky. Many Icelandic place names are comprised of common words smooshed together. So Snaefellsnes is 'Snow Mountain Peninsula' (*nes* means 'peninsula'); Reykjavík is 'Smoky Bay' and Eyjafjallajökull is 'Island Mountain Glacier'. Technically, it would be incorrect to write 'Snaefellsnes Peninsula', because that would be like writing 'peninsula peninsula'.

There are times, though, when clarity should trump pedantry. For example, the bay just north of Reykjavík is known as Faxaflói, where *flói* means 'bay' (*flói* is pronounced *floe-ee*). But there is no way the average English reader would know that Faxaflói is a bay, and so I call it Faxaflói Bay. The trickiest incidence of this is the suffix '–á', which means river. So Hvítá means white (*hvít*) river (*–á*). I call it the Hvítá river, knowing this means 'white river river', but trying not to care.

I sought out some colloquial Icelandic phrases to insert into my novels. There are some great ones.

My favourite is '*Hvalreki!*' which means 'Beached whale!' It's an expression of joy at good fortune, and refers to the glee an Icelander in times past would feel if he woke up one morning to find an enormous whale lying on the beach in front of his house. Whales provided massive quantities of meat and oil, which was very valuable before petroleum was discovered. It's the Icelandic equivalent of striking gold, and is used in a similarly metaphorical way as that expression.

Here are some others:

- *Laugardagur* – Saturday, literally hot tub day or washing day
- The big salmon – The big cheese
- Teaches the naked woman to spin – Necessity is the mother of invention
- Every man likes the smell of his own fart – Rather not think too much about this one
- Men do not limp while their legs are the same length – Don't fuss over my health
- Good to have a falcon in the corner – Who knows? Interior design tip?
- To play chess with the Pope – Go to the toilet
- It is better to be without trousers than without a book – Obvious, right?
- The dead lice are falling from my head – What a surprise!

- To lie under a fur – To spend a little time thinking. (Remember Thorgeir under his fur cloak trying to decide whether Iceland should be Christian a thousand years ago?)

One phrase that is often heard in Iceland is *'Thetta reddast'*, which means something between 'Everything is going to be OK' and 'It will sort itself out in the end'. It sums up Icelanders' optimism in the face of volcanoes, avalanches, financial meltdowns, and their entry not making it through to the final stages of the Eurovision song contest.

And, by and large, everything does turn out OK.

5 MAGNUS

I had my plot; now I needed a detective.

Creating your detective is probably the most important task for any writer when beginning a crime series. You want the man or woman to be interesting to you as much as to the reader. You want him (I decided on a man, perhaps because I am a man) to be sympathetic, strong, independent, intelligent. But to create drama he needs flaws: traits that will get him into trouble. He needs personal problems. He needs to be in conflict with family, friends or colleagues.

Given these requirements, you can see how writers have created detectives who are middle-aged, divorced, with a drink problem, a wayward daughter and a difficult boss. All that really helps with the drama, but it creates a new difficulty: a stereotype which the writer has to be careful not to follow too closely.

So I didn't start from that point. I had a particular problem. I needed a detective who spoke Icelandic, knew Iceland, yet could see his own country clearly through the eyes of a guest. Solve that, and I could add features that would make him interesting.

First, I needed a name. The name had to be easily recognizable to English speakers – Skarphédinns need not apply – simple to say and read, and authentically Icelandic. A name immediately popped into my head, and it may have popped into yours. Magnus.

For Britons of my generation, Magnus Magnusson was the best-known Icelander, although in fact he was born in Scotland to Icelandic parents and lived most of his life in Britain. He had a great name (Latin pun stumbled upon by accident). He presented the intellectual quiz show *Mastermind* on TV, and I remember his blue twinkling eyes and soft Scottish-Icelandic accent fondly.

Despite its Latin derivation, Magnus, or, as it is written in Icelandic, Magnús – pronounced Magnoos – is an authentic Icelandic name. The story as told to me goes that in the Middle Ages there was an Icelandic poet named Sigvatr at the court of a Norwegian king. The king had an illegitimate child born prematurely, and Sigvatr thought the baby was going to die immediately. The poet, not wanting to wake the king, hastily baptized the baby, giving him the name 'Magnus' after 'Carolus Magnus', the Latin name for Charlemagne, meaning Charles the Great. Magnus survived, grew strong and eventually became King Magnus of Norway himself.

So, like that Icelandic poet, I called my progeny 'Magnus'. Or at least, as described in Chapter Four, 'Magnus' when he is speaking English; it's 'Magnús' when he is speaking Icelandic. May he live long.

Back to the problem: how on earth do I get him to be a policeman capable of interviewing suspects in Icelandic and of seeing the country through a foreigner's eyes?

This is the answer I came up with after a couple of weeks' thought.

Magnus was born in Iceland to Icelandic parents. His father was an academic and his mother an alcoholic. When Magnus was eight, his parents split up. His father went to teach at university in Boston, and his mother kept Magnus and his little brother with her. Because of her alcoholism, Magnus lived at his grandparents' farm on Snaefellsnes in the west of the country. He had a miserable time.

Magnus's mother died when Magnus was twelve, and he and his little brother Óli went to join their father in Boston. So Magnus grew up in America, attended an American high school, but never forgot his Icelandic roots, or his native language.

When he was twenty, Magnus's father was murdered. The local police tried to solve the crime, but failed. Magnus tried, and also failed. But, as a result, after leaving university he decided to become a policeman.

Ten years later, he is the only homicide detective in America who speaks Icelandic. So when the Icelandic National Police Commissioner visits America looking to borrow a detective to help the Reykjavík police with modern crime, Magnus is his man, and he is invited back to Iceland. The day he lands in the country, an Icelandic professor is found murdered near Lake Thingvellir, and our story begins.

This background created a number of problems for Magnus, problems that I could explore in my future books. Could he understand Icelandic society, having been out of it for so long? Did he see himself as an Icelander or an American? As an American policeman used to carrying a gun, how did he deal with the tamer Icelandic criminal scene? How did he deal with being an outsider? How did he deal with Icelandic women? How did he come to terms with his parents' early death and his painful time at his grandparents' farm? And, a gift for a crime writer, who killed his father?

Plenty to work on there, and I am still working on it.

So, Magnus is an Icelander. But what are Icelanders really like?

Now, that is a dangerous question. Dangerous because we are in the territory of playing with stereotypes.

I first came across the notion of stereotype at school studying history. I think I had suggested that the First World War started because Germans liked invading people. I was admonished, quite rightly, and told that 'stereotypes' had no place in history. You couldn't say that Italians were excitable, the French didn't queue, the Americans were loud or that the Germans liked invading people. It was bad history, it was often plain wrong and it was morally dubious. All true.

And yet. It is hard to suggest that the unification of Germany or even the origins of the First World War can be analysed without some understanding of the development of Prussian militarism. I believe there are certain traits that are more prevalent in Iceland than elsewhere, and I think it is the job of a novelist to capture these. But a writer has to be careful. For many of the most obvious characteristics, there are less obvious, opposing trends lying just beneath the surface. Which makes it all the more interesting.

Some of what follows is based on my own observation. Much of it comes from Icelanders themselves speaking about their own country, especially some of those I have met in London, whose removal from home gives them some clarity. Many of these characteristics will be examined in future chapters.

Most of the character of Icelanders derives from their geography and history, which I have already touched upon:

dark cold winters, summer days of interminable length, poverty, rubbish weather, the struggle to grow food, a small society and centuries of dominance by a foreign absentee government.

Icelanders work hard, and they work quickly. I have already mentioned how most of them have several different jobs. Historically, there was a lot to get done during the short summer on the farm, and many daylight hours to do it in. If you didn't work all those hours, you starved in the winter. They are not good planners and they are not good timekeepers. If they say they will do something, they do it right away or not at all.

An example. When I emailed Pétur and asked him if he knew any policemen in Reykjavík I could talk to, I expected a response in a couple of days giving me the contact details of a friend's husband who was a cop. What I received was an email ten minutes later saying that the chief of the Reykjavík Metropolitan Police was expecting my call. Immediately. The police chief gave me a great contact whom I have met several times.

Another example. CrimeFest is an enjoyable literary festival for crime fiction which takes place in Bristol every May. In May 2013, a bunch of Icelandic crime writers were having a beer, and thinking: Wouldn't it be nice if there was a similar international crime festival in Reykjavík? Classic authors' chat in the bar. Except that in November that same year Iceland Noir held its first festival in Reykjavík, with top crime writers from all over the world showing up. I can't imagine a major literary festival being set up so quickly in any other country.

Speed helps in other ways. Icelanders take search and rescue seriously: there are 99 units with 3,500 volunteers. They have plenty of toys: snowmobiles, boats, super-jeeps with massive tyres, horses, even parachutes. They have always been willing to drop everything and set out in rough seas to help a ship in distress, or to rush up a mountain through a blizzard to look for a lost neighbour, or these days a lost tourist. This all plays to Icelanders' strengths: tough, brave, resourceful, quick to react, eager to play with man-toys. They are ready to respond to earthquakes, volcanic eruptions or flash floods at a moment's notice. They have found their niche in world disasters: they get there first. The Icelanders only have a small global emergency unit, but they pride themselves on being the first international response on the scene in places like Haiti.

I have mentioned that literature has always been important in Icelandic culture, and so too is art, music and sport. With a hard-working population, willing to put in the extra hours, some of it is very good. Reykjavík's bookshops are big, and groaning with books written by a small population. The city is teeming with art, some of it good, some of it bad, most of it quirky. Early in the evenings on Fridays and Saturdays the streets of downtown Reykjavík are full of bearded men unloading the musical equipment of dozens of groups ready to play their heart out.

The Icelanders love per capita comparisons, but the national achievements really are impressive for a place with a population similar to Coventry or Buffalo. World-class musicians include Björk, Sigur Rós and Of Monsters and Men. Iceland's opera singers, artists and designers spread across the globe. Dramas about sheep win international film awards. The football team reached the semi-finals of the Euros in 2016, and in Halldór Laxness Iceland had a winner of the Nobel Prize for Literature in 1955. After this victory, Icelanders crowed that they had the highest number of Nobel laureates per capita until they found out a guy from the Faroe Islands had won a Nobel Prize for medicine in 1903.

I sometimes think that there is a department at the University of Iceland devoted to calculating per capita statistics. These supposedly include: the most peaceful country, the highest internet usage, the greatest levels of gender equality, the highest literacy ratio, the most rules for writing poetry, the most Coca-Cola consumption, the most musicians, the most authors and the highest sales of the computer game *Championship Manager*. They also eat a lot of Cheerios and Cocoa Puffs, but I don't have the global statistics on those to hand.

There is something about the way Icelanders go about things that is effective, beyond just hard work. Like the great disrupters of Silicon Valley, they move fast and break things. They are optimists; when something goes wrong, they try something else. Sometimes this works. Sometimes it doesn't, but hey, *thetta reddast*.

Tucked into that per capita list was 'gender equality'. The generalization goes that women are tough, independent and well educated in Iceland. Although they are not paid the same as men, it is closer than in other countries. Iceland had the first elected female president, Vigdís Finnbogadóttir, who was elected in 1980. The success of women is ascribed by some to the fact that many were left alone to manage while their husbands went away to sea. Some say that having children early helps. Women will often have their first child while still at university, which means that when they are in their early thirties they have older children and are able to struggle on equal terms with men on the career ladder.

On Friday, 24 October 1975, Icelandic women went on strike for a day, refusing to go to work or to do any chores around the house or look after children. Ninety per cent of Icelandic women participated. The men prepared: employers bought paper and crayons in anticipation of kids joining their fathers at work, and easy-to-cook sausages sold out in the shops. The strike was successful: in 1976 Parliament passed a law guaranteeing equal pay.

And yet sexism is not unknown in Iceland. In 2018 a group of mostly male politicians were recorded by a fellow customer in the Klaustur Bar near Parliament discussing what they would like to do to their female colleagues, causing uproar and demands for resignations. Domestic abuse is still a real problem.

As is alcoholism. Many Icelanders are binge drinkers. They share this with many northern countries, places where winter nights are long. And, despite the extortionate prices, they somehow manage to get drunk at the weekend. Which, I have to admit, can be fun.

Icelandic families used to be large. Two parents, nine children and an extended family of cousins and aunts. When the parents were in trouble – the father lost at sea, for example – relatives would step in. Families are often large now, but in a different, more complex way. I mentioned that people have children young. They don't necessarily get married young, or get married at all. Many people get married several times to other people who already have children. A child may have several parents and step-parents, and a minibus full of siblings, step-siblings and half-siblings, and an aunt her own age. Grandmothers in their forties help out their daughters with childcare. It all seems to work, in fact it seems to work very well, but I wonder what effect – if any – this breakdown in the nucleus of the family has on children.

One of the global measures that Iceland seems to score

very highly is equality. And at first glance, it does seem to be a classic Nordic social democratic society where everyone respects everyone else, everyone calls everyone else by their first names, and everyone goes to school together. This derives from the shared hardship of a community of poor farmers and the historic lack of an aristocratic or governing class.

And yet, scratch beneath the surface . . . At the beginning of the twentieth century a small group of families, known as 'the Octopus', controlled trade into the country. They were rich, the rest of the Icelanders were poor, but they kept a low profile. These were joined and in some cases supplanted by a new generation of entrepreneurs and bankers in the 1990s and early 2000s, who rode the boom. They bought newspapers and some of their friends became politicians. When the bust came in 2008, known in Iceland as the *kreppa*, this group were badly bruised but survived. Many Icelanders are still resentful of them.

In a society where networks are so integral, cliques develop. My own experience of Iceland is that the bankers know the bankers and the writers know the writers, but they don't know each other, or not very well – although I do know one writer who is both. It's not a rigid class system on the classic British model. But it's not a social democratic paradise of equality either.

I mentioned how history can resonate in current Icelandic society. But one aspect of the past which seems for some reason to have left no trace is the thirst for blood of the Vikings. Icelanders are peaceable, at least when sober. The country has no army, and although Iceland is a member of NATO, joining caused mass demonstrations. Cynics might say they only joined for the money flowing from the

US air base at Keflavík. A young male culture which venerates toughness and strength when faced with nature does not produce enthusiastic soldiers, or anything more violent than the magnificent cry in unison of 'Huh!' with a thunderclap at Iceland football games. Apparently this isn't Viking at all, but was imported from Motherwell Football Club near Glasgow.

Icelanders can be rude behind the till in a shop and look as if they want to be somewhere else, but that's only because they are thinking through their chord change at the gig at the Kaffibarinn that evening. You might have been cut up by a guy in a jeep on his mobile phone with no indicator flashing, but he has things to do and people to see. Icelanders may never include you in a round of drinks in a bar, but that is only because they haven't had time to take out the mortgage to pay for it.

In my experience, Icelanders are warm, friendly, generous, kind, interesting, well-read and have the sharpest of senses of humour. And that's a generalization I am willing to stick by.

To understand Icelanders, I believe you need to understand Bjartur. Bjartur is the independent hero of Halldór Laxness's greatest novel, *Independent People*. The book is set at the beginning of the twentieth century. Over eighteen years as a shepherd, Bjartur saves the money to buy his own farm on some very marginal land. Bjartur's life is a struggle to eke a living out of this farm, called Summerhouses. He marries twice, faces starvation and destitution, but never gives up on his dream of remaining an independent farmer. He is stubborn to the point of cruelty. He is also a poet and sensitive to the folklore around him.

· · ·

Why make Magnus American and not English? He could easily be a detective from Scotland Yard, who had been sent to England as a child.

I considered this initially. But as I began to understand Icelanders, I realized Britain wouldn't work as well as America. Icelanders fit in very well in London, and a London detective would have little trouble fitting in to Iceland. The irony, the reserve, the reluctance to use guns: that would all seem familiar. It seemed to me that an American homicide detective would notice more differences, and would have a harder time fitting in, which would make for a more interesting series of novels.

Understanding Magnus's American background and experiences brought its own challenges. I don't make life easy for myself.

So, I had my detective. I had my plot. I had studied the language, spoken to Icelanders in London and read widely about the country.

It was time to go there.

6 TIME TO GO

This visit to Iceland was going to be very different from my book tour in 1995. This time I had to build up a store of the impressions, the feelings, the sounds, the smells and the little details to fuel my writing of the first draft of my novel over a six-month period. I had researched many settings for my previous novels – Fife, Brazil, Massachusetts, Prague, Clerkenwell, the Côte d'Azur, Wyoming, South Africa and 1930s Berlin – so I knew what I was doing, but I was daunted. Before, most of my characters had been flying in and out of places. This time Magnus and my characters were stuck in Iceland for at least three books, maybe more.

I had better get it right.

Over the years, I have developed and refined a method for gathering information on locations for my books. I wander around with a tape recorder, a camera and a notebook, my eyes and ears on high alert, taking note of anything I see or hear that might be useful. I use the tape recorder most, muttering into it thoughts and impressions as they occur to me. My wife finds this mildly embarrassing. I remember a trip to Prague where she chose to walk a couple of yards behind me, pretending she had nothing to do with the weird English guy talking to himself.

It may look weird – it does look weird – but it works. I do listen to the recording at the end of the day and write most of it down, but it is the act of speaking the thought into the recorder that fixes it into my memory.

What am I looking for? Anything and everything, but there are a few areas I focus on.

First impressions. You only get these once. Write them down.

Details. When I started writing I used to worry that I would be lousy at description because I am not a natural at metaphor or simile, and my prose is clear rather than purple. But I learned that great descriptions often are made up of perfectly selected small details. These are best when they don't match the stereotypes of the location. For example, Copacabana beach is famous for its beautiful sunbathers and its sparkling sea. When I was there, drinking a caipirinha with a friend, a hooker with bright yellow hair lurched up to us, and after propositioning us, threw up on a nearby lamp post. That went into the book, as did the small boy peeing on a police car parked in the shade of a palm tree.

Symbols. I look for prominent landmarks in a location that I will refer to several times in a book. Each repetition makes the landmark and hence the location seem more familiar to the reader, so that by the end of the book she feels she really knows the location. Ideally, these will not be the tourist stereotypes that come to mind immediately when you think of a place, but in practice this is hard to avoid. It's good if the symbol can be looked at in different ways by different people at different times of day. In Rio, the obvious choice is the Corcovado, with the statue of Christ the

Redeemer on top of the mountain overlooking the city. But more interesting is the favela that tumbles down to the sea on the headland between Ipanema and Copacabana beaches. It is both squalid and beautiful: a sign of modern poverty and almost medieval in its primitive construction.

People. I will need to describe people in each setting, and it is useful to have a set of descriptions to start with. Once again, the less stereotypical the better, but at this stage it's important to write down what you see, and stereotypes do wander around the streets of the countries that created them. There are indeed beach beauties in Rio, and incredibly skilful young men playing foot volleyball on the beach, but there are also bald plump men with glasses and briefcases.

Movement. What moves? Description comes alive if it isn't static. People, vehicles, birds, clouds, animals all move about, come and go. A street kid looking skinny on the pavement is one thing. A street kid peeing on the local police car is a better thing – at least for the novelist.

Sounds and smells. What can you hear? What can you smell? Stop, shut your eyes and wait. Then write it down. I remember lying on a beach in Rio, with my eyes closed and listening. It sounded as if I was in a bar. People go to beaches in Rio not just to get a tan, certainly not to read a book, but to chat, to see and be seen, to exchange gossip.

Enough of my arduous research trip to Rio. For better or worse I had decided to write several books in a city with appalling weather: Reykjavík. I have looked back at my notes on this trip in May of 2008, and these were my rather disjointed first impressions.

It's small and northern. Despite the cloud, there is a feeling of lightness about the place. Most of Reykjavík is in shades of grey, many of them light grey, brightened by a number of small houses with brightly coloured metal roofs. It's a hip, fashion-conscious city, yet innocent at the same time, clean, easy to walk around. Although many streets are narrow, you can usually see some distance to the sea and mountains, so it doesn't feel cramped. It's friendly in rather a repressed way. The air is fresh and cool, with an occasional hint of sulphur. There is not much smell of traffic. The main sounds are the hum, not the roar, of traffic, the laugh or yelp of a human, the muffled bass line coming out of a car or bar, the clank of construction equipment and the occasional cry of a seabird. The sky changes constantly as clouds mix and merge with the sun, performing a kind of bridal dance: you catch glimpses of lighter grey and sometimes bright blue. It rains and then it stops. The few trees are short, unhappy and just budding. A few stubby daffodils are still blooming in May. The temperature is cool: 8 °C, and at this time of year it doesn't get dark until 10.30 p.m.

Movement and details. Steam rising from a road junction – perhaps a leak in the underground geothermal heating system? A bright yellow Mustang convertible. A girl wobbling on a bike wearing a lime-green top, a leopard-skin skirt and a tail. A man pushing a baby round and round the city – I saw him several times. Two doughty tourists walking through the main shopping street in hiking gear. A class of kids in the Parliament Square, all with fair hair apart from one East Asian girl.

What are the smells of Reykjavík? There is an impression of cleanliness, although I'm told the pollution from cars is worse than a visitor might assume. When the wind is from the harbour, you can smell fish. And when the wind is from the south-east, you can smell sulphur, leaking out from the centre of the earth at the geothermal power station thirty kilometres away.

I needed symbols of Reykjavík, and there were two obvious candidates, both of which have recurred frequently in my novels. The first is Mount Esja. This is a large, long, muscular ridge of crenelated rock and snow that lies to the north of Reykjavík, on the other side of a smooth grey fjord dotted with islands. You can see glimpses of it from many places in town. It changes constantly, with the seasons, the weather and even the time of day. It can glow pink, glisten yellow, gleam white and brood black. On some days its grey wrinkles can be clearly made out in the sunshine under a blue sky. Tiny clouds can hover just above the flat summit, larger cumulus plunge and soar above it, or heavy grey blankets of moisture bear down, leaving only the foothills showing. It can look beautiful or ominous, or sometimes both at once. It has become an old friend, a friend with ever-changing moods.

The second is the Hallgrímskirkja, or 'Hallgrímur's Church'. A hill rises above the centre of Reykjavík, and on top of this hill stands the Hallgrímskirkja, the largest church in Iceland. Despite its size, it's not a cathedral: that is an older, much smaller building near the Parliament Square. Inside, it's very warm, unlike any English church I have ever been to. From the top of its spire you get a marvellous view over Reykjavík, the sea that surrounds the city on three sides and, beyond that, the mountains. But it's not the view *from* it that is important, it's the view *of* it.

The church was designed in the 1930s and built between 1945 and 1986. It is constructed out of smooth concrete. The spire, supported by swept-back wings, swoops upwards to dominate the town. You see it from afar as you approach Reykjavík, and you see it as you walk the streets downtown. It can glow soft and yellow in low evening light, or loom grey and brutal in the drizzle. It has a kind of smooth grace to it, but it's also austere, depending how you are feeling. Some of my characters think it looks like an intercontinental ballistic missile. Some of them think it looks like a space rocket. One of them thinks it looks like a penis.

People. I identified a number of distinct 'types' among the people I saw on that first trip. I wouldn't say that this is a definitive taxonomy of Icelanders at all, merely a snapshot of some of those I saw in 2008, and I fear some of my descriptions are not very kind.

Old guys who think of themselves as cool: long greying curly hair, bushy beard or raffish moustaches, leather jacket, broad-rimmed hat and a scarf tied just so. Big guys, square shoulders, blond, with stubble on their cheeks and stubble on their scalps, wearing black leather jackets. Thin guys with straggly red hair and thin straggly facial hair, woolly hats and jeans that sag and straggle. Big, broad, pasty-faced men, with thin fair hair, acne, a paunch and a couple of breasts. Little neat bird-like men with thick silver hair brushed back Soviet-style, weather-beaten faces and bright blue twinkling eyes. Young men wearing T-shirts under expensive sweaters, jeans, leather shoes, thick fair hair brushed back and oiled, neat designer stubble and thin metal glasses.

Tall, long-limbed women with blonde hair, fair complexion, blue eyes, white smile, striding with an air of confidence but not unapproachable. Thin small women with pale skin, blue eyes and black hair. What look like farm girls: hefty, broad pasty face, bad skin, upturned piggy nose, looking unsophisticated and innocent. Middle-aged women with black hair, bright lipstick, mascara and leather trousers. Thin middle-aged woman with red collar-length hair, glasses, pale slightly freckled skin and blue intelligent eyes.

After a full afternoon of muttering into my tape recorder, I headed to my hotel. The Leifur Eiríksson is situated at the top of the hill right opposite the Hallgrímskirkja. Between the hotel and the church stands a fine statue of Leifur Eiríksson, the son of Erik the Red of Greenland fame, who sailed from Greenland to discover America. He is clutching a battleaxe and striding westwards across the city beneath him towards Canada.

My room had a nice view of Leif. I diligently wrote up my notes of the day's sightings and then set out for a night on the town. Reykjavík is famous for its raucous nightlife, it was Saturday, and I needed to do my research. I found a bar, ordered a burger, and drank a beer. Quickly. I ordered another one.

The bar was barely a quarter full. It was eight thirty. I had another beer. It had been a large burger. The beer was yellow and gassy. My stomach was full and I was tired. And the bar was still three-quarters empty.

Sometimes I really enjoy a long slow pint in a bar by myself. Sometimes I just get impatient. This was one of those impatient evenings. At nine thirty I concluded that the stuff about Reykjavík nightlife I had read was overblown hype. At nine forty-five I left the bar and looked for somewhere else more lively. The streets were more or less empty, although there was a parade of fancy cars on the main shopping street, Laugavegur.

I gave up and went to bed.

The curtains were thin, and it was not yet dark, so it

took me a while to go to sleep. I was woken at about midnight by laughter and shouting. For the next three or four hours the clamour rose, until it sounded as if there was a riot going on not far from my hotel. I knew I should have got up and checked it all out. But I was feeling tired, foolish and a little middle-aged. I read a book for half an hour and eventually went back to sleep.

FAVOURITE PLACES - THINGHOLT

By 'Thingholt', I mean the bloody great hill in the middle of Reykjavík with a church on top. I assume that in Viking times they held a *thing* here, meaning an assembly. It's bordered by the Tjörnin pond on the west, Laugavegur to the north, the National Hospital to the east and the City Airport to the south. It's a residential area bang in the middle of town, full of small houses with brightly painted corrugated iron roofs – predominantly red, but also green and blue. The walls are either concrete or corrugated iron, and many are brightly painted too.

Most of the houses with corrugated metal walls were built between 1880 and 1925. The rain in Reykjavík frequently falls horizontally, so wooden walls tended to rot. Wood was also expensive, since it all had to be imported, and it burns: much of Reykjavík burned down in 1915. Corrugated iron was all the rage until the Icelanders discovered concrete in the 1920s.

The dwellings are small, with little gables and tiny gardens behind picket fences. The place is delightfully, domestically, quiet; the roads are too narrow for Reykjavík's traffic to make much headway. There are primary schools and playgrounds, corner shops and bicycles.

The western slope, rising up from the Tjörnin, seems to have the oldest houses, built by Reykjavík merchants in the nineteenth century. Old in Thingholt means quaint rather than grand. The houses to the south are a little grander; this is where the Reykjavík bigwigs live, and you might spot the odd security camera. The slope to the north above Laugavegur is hipper and quirkier, and to the east it is a bit scruffier. This is where Magnus lives. I was told that Thingholt would be a little too bohemian for a policeman, so I had him lodge with one of his colleagues' punkish sister. Their house is a lovely small white building with a steep red corrugated roof on Njálsgata – I know exactly which one. No one can quite agree where precisely Thingholt's borders run, but according to the more pedantic residents Njálsgata may lie just outside its limits. Which sounds about right for Magnus.

When Julian Assange and his colleagues from Wikileaks came to Iceland to edit the video of an American operation in Iraq which had been leaked to them, they stayed in a house in Thingholt. My third Magnus novel, *Meltwater*, features a similar outfit who also holed up in a little house on the hill.

I have mentioned the terrific view from the top of the Hallgrímskirkja, but the views snatched strolling around the hill are perhaps better because more unexpected. Between a child's swing and a rowan tree, you suddenly catch a glimpse of Mount Esja, or the Tjörnin, or the Pearl – the water tower to the south of town – or much closer, the swooping spire of the church itself.

Skólavördustígur is a road that heads straight uphill to the Hallgrímskirkja from the bottom of Laugavegur. The name is a mouthful, an effort to read, let alone pronounce, so think of it as the Skola Street. This is where you catch the best view of the church, always shifting with the time of day and the weather. The street itself is lined with galleries, some unashamedly touristy, but some selling pieces that are fascinating, quirky, stunning or all three. The various rocks, metals and glass spewed up by Iceland's volcanoes are popular materials, as is fish-skin leather. The Handknitting Association of Iceland, up the hill on the left, contains an extraordinary collection of wool garments, including the famous *lopapeysa* sweaters. These are made of wool from Icelandic sheep that have two layers, a wet-resistant outer layer and an insulating inner layer. The sweaters are warm and weatherproof, but sell for the kind of price that prompts you to consider selling your firstborn in order to clothe your secondborn, or vice versa.

I checked out Reykjavík. I was looking for places people might live, places people might meet, and the odd place someone might get stabbed or shot. It's a bit morbid, but it's my job. I was to revisit all the spots I saw on this first trip many times over the following ten years. In May 2008, the global financial crash was just beginning its downward lurch. It was to hit Iceland particularly hard over the following twelve months.

I started where Ingólfur Arnarson started, in Austurvöllur Square, which is a couple of hundred yards south of the bay and in the middle of what is now known as 'Downtown'. Austurvöllur is a bit of a mouthful, so let's call it the Parliament Square, since Parliament is on one side. If you think Reykjavík is small for a capital city now, this is where you realize how seriously small it used to be a hundred years ago. The square is a patch of green with a statue of a politician in the middle, some scrappy grass and daffodils and a few benches. The Parliament building itself looks like the town hall of a small Yorkshire town, complete with blackened stone. And, of course, a hundred years ago Reykjavík was the same size as a small Yorkshire town.

The square has seen some action. A year after I visited for the first time it was the site of the 'pots-and-pans' revolution, when 5 per cent of the country's population crowded into the square and banged crockery to demand change. It worked – more on that in Chapter Eleven.

On another side of the square is the Hótel Borg, which was for a long time Reykjavík's only posh hotel. It was built by a famous Icelandic strongman in the 1930s – when they say that I assume they mean he financed it, but maybe he used his own hands. It's grand in an understated art deco way, and a perfect place for my wealthy Tolkien-besotted American character to stay while he is visiting Reykjavík. On a third side of the square is the Café Paris, which is a place to see Iceland's great and good, and an excellent place for lunch and a coffee. Politicians are frequent patrons, although, given the scandal I mentioned in Chapter Five, you may want to avoid listening in too closely to their conversations.

Just to the south of the Parliament Square is the Tjörnin, a large pond about a kilometre in length, access to which presumably attracted Ingólfur to this spot. (By the way, although I call it 'the Tjörnin', I really shouldn't, since the '–in' at the end of 'Tjörnin' already means 'the', so I am calling it 'the the Tjörn'. It's just one of those little things I like to do to annoy Icelanders. Tjörn just means 'pond' anyway.) This is not a man-made municipal water feature, but an important natural international transport hub. There is Keflavík International Airport, there is the City Airport in the middle of Reykjavík, and then there is the Tjörnin. It is the westernmost body of fresh water in Iceland, and hence a popular stopping-off point for birds on their migration.

Swans, geese, ducks, terns, seagulls and a host of complicated species known only to twitchers paddle and fuss, refuelling for the next leg of their journey.

The modern Reykjavík town hall leans out over the lake. It's worth a quick visit, especially on your return from a trip around the countryside, which you can trace on a massive model of a relief map of Iceland inside.

To the north-west of the Parliament Square is the Old Harbour, which used to be the only harbour until they built a new one for freight further east, but is still used by fishing boats. Reykjavík is still a serious fishing port and there is always a lot going on.

Tucked away near the water, in a patch of land which has been under intermittent construction for the last ten years, is Baejarins Beztu Pylsur, a red hot-dog stand with a picture of Bill Clinton stuffing his face outside it. It is just a hot-dog stand in a car park, but there is usually a queue, and although I think it's a bit overblown to claim that the hot dogs are the best per capita hot dogs in the world, they do taste good. One way or another, whenever I go to Iceland I seem to stop there. For the truly authentic Reykjavík experience it should be drizzling lightly.

The stand had a narrow escape recently. A nearby crane fell, just missed the stand, but destroyed a bench nearby a few seconds after two girls had finished their hot dogs and left it.

As I walked along the edge of the bay eastwards, I passed a massive construction site. This was a planned concert hall, which cost a huge amount of money and was nearly cancelled during the financial crisis, but fortunately wasn't. It's now finished, it's called Harpa, and it's beautiful. It's like a large cubic jewel, gleaming and glimmering in greens, yellows, blues and purples. The façade was designed by the Icelandic artist Ólafur Elíasson, and is made out of glass bricks that reflect and refract sunlight so that the interior is always changing during the day, and at night is stunningly illuminated. Go inside and gawp.

The bay itself is known as Faxaflói and faces north. To the north-east loom the flanks of Esja. Far to the north, and I mean a hundred kilometres away, is Snaefellsnes, a peninsula that juts out to the west of Iceland. At the very end of this stands the volcano Snaefellsjökull, a perfect cone topped with an ice-cream glacier. On a clear day you can see it from Reykjavík, hovering above the water in the distance.

Along the edge of the bay stands a row of tall apartment blocks. In 2008 they were only half built, and construction stopped for a few years during the crash. The area is known as the 'Shadow District', and I decided it was an ideal place for a yuppy banker in my second novel to live. And there were some deserted narrow streets running between the buildings which would be great places for him to be attacked. Very useful.

The police station is close to the bay, and in fact there is a good view from Magnus's desk over to Snaefellsnes. The National Police Commissioner's office is right on the bay too. But the area around the police station, known as Hlemmur, is a bit scruffy: bus station, tattoo parlours, dodgy shops, needles in back alleys. During the crash, there were squats around here, and if you were to meet a strung-out junky in central Reykjavík, it would probably be around Hlemmur. It would be inaccurate to suggest it feels unsafe; all city centres have their scruffier parts, and this is, or was, Reykjavík's.

Walking further east along the bay, I came to the Höfdi House. This is a white mansion standing in its own lawn by the side of the water. Icelanders don't really do mansions: even rich people's houses are small by international mansion standards, as indeed is the Höfdi House. But it was the smartest house in town in the first half of the century, and was nabbed by the British government for their consulate. The house had a ghost, named Sóley, who drove the British out and they sold the place in 1952. Thirty years later it became the site of the famous disarmament talks between Reagan and Gorbachev. Apparently the Russian delegates enjoyed watching *Tom and Jerry* cartoons in the basement: Russians didn't get *Tom and Jerry* in Moscow in those days. It is now owned by the city, and is used for official functions.

Seemed to me a good spot for my characters to choose to meet.

Further on to the east, I came to Iceland's equivalent to Wall Street, Borgartún. This is a straight road running parallel to the bay, lined with modern office buildings of glass and red and black stone a few storeys high. *Vanity Fair* describes the style as 'Asshole Capitalist', but I think that's a little harsh. Every capital city needs somewhere to put its banks, and with its views of Mount Esja and Faxaflói Bay and its manageably sized buildings, I suspect this would be a pretty good place to work. And for Magnus to meet a hotshot lawyer.

I walked back along Laugavegur, which is Reykjavík's smartest shopping street. *Laug* means 'hot spring', so this was the road from Ingólfur's original Norse settlement to the geothermal spring, which is now a swimming pool with hot tubs near Borgartún. It became the route women took to do their washing, and presumably a crowded thoroughfare on Saturday, or *laugardagur*, when everyone went off for a bath. It's still a hot place on Saturday night, after my bedtime, since most of the trendy clubs and bars are on this street.

The trendiest of these is Kaffibarinn. This is a small metal town house, painted bright red, a few yards up Bergstadastraeti from Laugavegur. It is easily identifiable by the London Underground sign hung above the door. It has an awesome reputation: *the* place to go on a weekend night for music and violent dancing. It's supposed to be or have been part-owned by Damon Albarn of Blur, but it's hard to pin that factoid down: maybe he had a drink there once. Iceland's most famous film director, Baltasar Kormákur, met Hallgrímur Helgason at the bar there, and decided to make a film of his book, *101 Reykjavík*.

The bar itself is a very pleasant place to go during the day, or an early weekday evening. Warm, cosy, wooden, old, with trendily dressed and laid-back bar staff. By night, things change, as I found out several years later.

I went to dinner at Pétur's house one Saturday. I told him and his guests I planned to go to some clubs afterwards for research purposes. Dinner was wonderful, but it dragged on, and we all drank quite a bit. I assumed everyone had forgotten about my plan. Finally, at 2.30 a.m., an author there announced it was time to go to Kaffibarinn.

It was a bewildering experience. The music was loud, the beat insistent – fair enough. The room at the back was heaving with a mass of bodies, mostly Icelandic, all drunk or high, swaying and writhing. It was summer – at 3 a.m. it was dawn or dusk or something – and the dim daylight seemed to give everyone an illicit energy. Inside, elbows and feet were jabbing. Outside, there was much shouting, swearing, baring of stomachs and chests, and vomiting. We left after an hour or so, because one of our group was embarrassed at jostling into her students.

I found it extremely interesting, but it would be wrong to say I enjoyed it. I'm way too old.

But I do like a scruffy pub, and I thought Magnus would like one too. Two Icelanders in London had recommended I try the Grand Rokk, which lurked off Hverfisgata between Laugavegur and the bay. Sadly, this place is no longer open. To get in, you went through a white picket gate in a white picket fence past a small outside tent for smokers. Inside, the bar was wood panelled, cosy and smelled strongly of spilled beer. A row of steady drinkers lined the bar: two old guys with grey hair and flat caps, a red-faced man with a bushy beard, a chubby American girl with short blonde hair and a chubby Icelandic friend, a Filipina and a shaven-headed Swedish guy in leathers. They all seemed to know each other, and the conversation was general and amiable in a mix of Icelandic and English. The older guys had shot glasses of spirits to chase their beers. A few feet away from the bar two men were playing chess. A particularly ruddy drinker suddenly started singing 'Summertime' from *Porgy and Bess* in a rich, sensuously slurred baritone. Everyone ignored him.

A good bolthole for Magnus.

Sadly, the Grand Rokk went bankrupt and is closed now. If you want to see the clientele, they have moved on to 46 on Hverfisgata, also known as the Gallery. This is not nearly as cosy as the Grand Rokk, and the large works of art on the walls seem out of step with its regulars. But the locals are still friendly. A warning: one or two of them might be drunk.

A city isn't just its centre. I needed to get outside to the suburbs; that is after all where most of the people live and much of the crime is committed. So I spent a couple of days on buses. The Reykjavík bus system isn't too difficult to figure out, and the drivers are helpful. It's great for people-watching: it seemed to me that many ordinary Icelanders looked a lot like ordinary Britons, or, to be more accurate, ordinary Scots. I was reminded of all that British and Irish DNA in the Icelandic genome.

The centre of Reykjavík has character, the outskirts don't. The town has grown rapidly in the last fifty years, swallowing up the farms that surrounded it in uniform housing estates. There is an inner ring of housing built in the fifties and sixties, which now has a kind of grey pebbledash East German retro charm. Some of the fancier houses in the suburbs show signs of architectural imagination, but, frankly, not many. Oddly, there are some stunning modern churches, for example at Mjódd and Grafarholt. But the suburbs are also infested with dual carriageways, car dealerships, DIY stores, IKEA, small squat office blocks and billboards.

Some of the developments were under construction, some more had been abandoned half built. The crash was coming. The only difference between Reykjavík's dull suburbs and those of its American or European equivalents are the stunning views: of Faxaflói Bay and its islands, of Mount Esja, of the heath and mountains to the south, and of the dramatic black lavascape stretching towards Keflavík to the west.

If there is a tough suburb of Reykjavík, it is Breidholt. This is where rich men say they grew up in rags-to-riches stories, it's where drug dealers live in novels and where people are interviewed about poverty in magazine articles. It all looked quite pleasant to me. It's a reminder that high-crime areas in Iceland don't resemble Baltimore, or Chicago's South Side, or the Moss Side in Manchester or

Harlesden in London. Frankly, the East Anglian town of King's Lynn is scarier, and King's Lynn is not very scary.

Breidholt has its gangsta rappers. One of them, Móri, describes life in Reykjavík's grittiest streets:

> I've been around. I've seen the darker side of life. I lived in Breidholt for a while. There is a drug dealer in every house there. There was also a gunfight there last year. But now I live in a nice area with my girlfriend and my pet turtle. I used to have two pet turtles but one of them died after the police raided my house and forgot to feed it. They didn't even have a warrant.

At the other end of the social scale is Seltjarnarnes, a neighbourhood just to the north-west of Reykjavík, sitting on a peninsula (a *nes*) jutting out into the bay. It's flat and windswept, but there are some wealthy roads here, many of the houses on which were bought by the 'quota kings' I discuss in Chapter Twelve, fishermen who made a killing by selling their fishing quotas. Some of the new breed of entrepreneurs live here too. One of these wealthy streets is named Bakkavör, which is also the name of a large food company now headquartered in London and founded by two Icelandic brothers. The houses themselves are modern and nicely designed, but not large. They look nowhere near as impressive as similar rich neighbourhoods in other capital cities, but that is in itself impressive. At least to me.

At the tip of Seltjarnarnes is the lighthouse and beach of Grótta . . .

FAVOURITE PLACES – GRÓTTA

What you think of Grótta depends on the intersection of your mood and the weather. If you are feeling tired or impatient and the wind is blowing and it's cold and raining and you can't see for more than five hundred metres, then Grótta can be a bust. But when it is calm and still, and it is warm enough to sit and stare, and the sun is taking its sweet time to duck below the horizon, it is a special place.

The name Grótta refers to a tiny island at the tip of Seltjarnarnes, on which a lighthouse stands. On the west side of this tip is a beach of black stones. At sunset, the sea shimmers in silver, gold, yellow, orange and even green as the sun creates a path heading westwards to the Atlantic and beyond. On a clear day, the snowy cone of Snaefellsjökull shimmers far away to the north. Sleek black cormorants slip in and out of the water and multicoloured ducks paddle about their business. Terns wheel and dive, letting out their distinctive cry of 'kría', which is their name in Icelandic. During nesting season, they can become quite aggressive; they will dive-bomb you if they decide you are in the wrong place.

Grótta can be dramatic, when the wind whips up the sea and waves crash on the rocks and the lighthouse, and sinister, when white fingers of fog caress the black volcanic stone.

There are many more dramatic and desolate beaches in Iceland, but the beauty of Grótta is it is so close to the centre of Reykjavík and yet so peaceful. A place to put down your notebook and tape recorder, and let your mind drift.

8 CRIME

By far my most important appointment on that first research trip to Reykjavík was with my police contact, Páll. Some very successful crime writers get by without worrying at all about police procedure – Agatha Christie springs to mind – but there are many other more modern examples. Others are obsessive, like Peter James. I had always aimed to get the details right in my financial thrillers, and I wanted to do the same in these Magnus mysteries, if only to create as vivid a portrait as I could of Iceland.

I am not a total slave to police procedure. Here are two examples that I have been happy to ignore or at least downplay in my books. Modern major investigations in Britain don't really involve a brilliant detective and his trusty sidekick interviewing everyone and then confronting the suspect in a lonely house somewhere. There are massive teams, coordinated by a computer, with patient analysis of forensic data, countless pointless interviews, endless watching nothing happen on CCTV footage, and keyword analysis of the inane chatter on the phones and computers of everyone involved. In the US, many detectives don't even interview their chief suspects until they have conclusive proof of their guilt, and even then they might not go for a confession. Confessions just give opportunities for defence lawyers to attack evidence. No tense confrontations and dramatic admissions. Most suspects don't say anything anyway; their lawyers have told them not to. These inconvenient modern methods make crime investigations much less dramatic, which is why I usually ignore them. But if I find an authentic and little-known detail of police methods, I will happily slip it in.

It's always useful to have a police contact wherever you are, but you can manage without in the US and Britain, where there are plenty of books that describe police procedures: my favourite is the 1,296-page *Practical Homicide Investigation* by Vernon J. Geberth. Unsurprisingly, there are none in Iceland, although a close reading of detective novels gives a few clues. I knew I needed a police contact; he had to be helpful; I had to ask the right questions and to note down the answers.

Being an Icelander, Páll wouldn't commit himself to a meeting following the email I had sent him two weeks before. This wouldn't bother me now, but it caused me no end of worry at the time. To my great relief, on the Sunday morning of my trip he agreed to meet me at police headquarters the next day.

Reykjavík's Metropolitan Police Headquarters is a dull grey box of a building opposite the Hlemmur bus station at the eastern end of Hverfisgata. There was still a smell of urine and vomit lying beneath disinfectant about the cells a day after the weekend rush hour. A Harley Davidson motorbike perched proudly on the landing on the first floor, and a lovely full-size snooker table took centre stage in the recreation room, a gift to the police from the British Army when it left Iceland during the war. One side of the building looks out over the bus station, the other on Mount Esja and the bay, at least from the top floors. Otherwise, this is a typical police station with computers, telephones, photocopiers, box files, public-safety posters, coffee machines and bland interview rooms.

Páll was a softly spoken man about my age, tall and balding. He seemed intelligent and empathetic. He went to high school with a boy who was to become Iceland's top crime writer, then to university and, after a spell in the police, he studied for a masters in America in criminology. He was a perfect source of information for me and extremely helpful. He looked like a schoolteacher, of the modern slightly left-wing variety rather than the old-fashioned authoritarian: not a stereotype of a policeman at all. I suspect he is very good at his job.

There is an obvious difficulty in writing a murder mystery set in Iceland: there is not much murder. Between 1980 and 2015, there were 56 murders in Iceland, which works out at 1.6 per year or 0.5 per 100,000 people per year. That's low, but not ultra-low. The UK currently averages 1.2 per 100,000; the US is much higher at 5.4. But two murders a year is not many. And, according to Páll, most murders are not that difficult to solve. Gunni is blind drunk and angry in a bar. He breaks a bottle and swings it at Siggi, cutting and killing him. When the police arrive, Gunni yells, 'Keep away or I'll kill you too.' Not really one for Hercule Poirot, or even Magnus.

Was it even realistic to set a crime series in Iceland? I dithered. But then I considered Oxford and Inspector Morse. Oxford has about half the population of Iceland, which, assuming the same murder rate as the rest of the UK, implies one or two murders per year. Colin Dexter wrote dozens of novels set in the city, and Morse and his sidekick Lewis appeared in at least sixty TV episodes, each including two or three unlikely killings. Colin Dexter and ITV got away with it, so I think Magnus and I can too.

I was looking for two things from Páll: the details of how the police would undertake an investigation from the discovery of the body to the eventual conviction of the murderer, and what difference Magnus would notice to homicide investigations back home.

Icelandic police have a friendly, almost cuddly image, especially when compared to their American counterparts. They have become experts at Instagram and Facebook, on which they rescue kittens and perform weird dances. It is an entirely different experience being stopped by an Icelandic traffic cop with her helpful smile and bobbing blonde ponytail, than by a shaven-headed American policeman with peak cap, sunglasses, jackboots, a gun wobbling at his hip and that special unsmiling look that asserts authority and, occasionally, fear.

In 2009, the Icelandic police lost their weekend leave when they spent every Saturday protecting Parliament during the pots-and-pans protests. These occasionally turned violent, in a not-very-scary Icelandic fashion. The police mostly showed restraint, although they sometimes fired tear gas. There was a lump in Páll's throat a couple of years later when he told me how peaceful protesters had formed a line to protect the police from the skyr – an Icelandic pseudo-yoghurt – and flagstones thrown at them by a minority of troublemakers.

Yet there are differences between the Icelandic and American (and British) way of doing things, and they don't always put the Icelanders in a good light.

Fortunately, the Icelanders have finally scrapped the

law permitting the murder of any Turk in Iceland, which had been enacted following the Barbary pirates' slave raids in the seventeenth century. In 1992 the law was repealed at the insistence of the visiting Turkish national handball team, and you can see their point. It did give the home team an unfair advantage.

The US and, to a lesser degree, the UK set great store in a suspect's right to remain silent, and in his right to a lawyer to tell him to remain silent. There are also restrictions on how long a suspect can remain in custody without being charged. The result of this is that investigators will often wait before charging a suspect until they have built a strong case against him.

Iceland has rules of arrest and evidence too; they are just different. When an investigator arrests a likely suspect, he interviews him, usually without a lawyer present. If he thinks the suspect is guilty, he will then get a warrant from a judge to keep the suspect in custody in solitary confinement for three weeks. This is known as the 'hot period', when the bulk of the investigation takes place. After three weeks, and only then, the police are required to show their evidence to the defence lawyer, and to ask the judge for an extension, should they require one. The standard technique is to let the suspect sweat it out in solitary for two and a half weeks, and then suggest they confess. Apparently, they usually do.

I visited Iceland's main prison once – I was planning a novel where Magnus would wind up in jail as a suspect for a couple of weeks. Litla-Hraun looms over the outskirts of the small coastal town of Eyrarbakki, about an hour south of Reykjavík. I was shown around by a tall, softly spoken, broad-shouldered warder named Hilmir. There are three wings for the permanent residents, and they are remarkably civilized. The communal kitchens are clean, each with a widescreen TV; the cells have en-suite showers and computers, although no internet. The inmates appeared cheery and friendly. I saw a class of three men doing an online university degree: those three securing Iceland's place at the top of the global rankings for per capita prison population in tertiary education. It reminded me a little of my daughter's hall of residence at university in England.

Those were three of the wings. The fourth, actually known as House No. 1, is for remand prisoners, in other words those who have not yet been found guilty. I saw some of this: individual cells with an internal high-walled courtyard with a plastic roof, around which prisoners are allowed to walk one hour of twenty-four. Hilmir was going to show me some of the prisoners, but one of them was going 'bananas'. It's a bit of a problem, apparently, prisoners in that wing going 'bananas'. To be fair to Hilmir, his use of that word in English should not be used against him, and he did seem genuinely very concerned with his charges' mental health. Nevertheless, I got the impression that suspects who were still assumed innocent were thrown into unpleasant solitary confinement. If they confessed, they got to move to the rather pleasant accommodation next door for a few months or years: prison terms in Iceland are low by international standards.

Hilmir told me there is a waiting list for Litla-Hraun.

It seems to me that, to work, this system relies on the fairness and integrity of Iceland's police and prosecutors. But, as in any country, the police are not always fair. Iceland's most notorious case of wrongful arrest involved what was probably a false confession. In 1974, two men, Gudmundur and Geirfinnur, disappeared from Hafnarfjördur, a town to the south-west of Reykjavík near the lava field. Six suspects were arrested, kept in solitary and interrogated. They confessed and were convicted. Over the years, there has been significant criticism of the investigation, and in 2018 five of the six were acquitted. A German security expert from Hamburg was drafted in to help with the original case, and some blame him for the miscarriage of justice. Memories of this case are still strong in Iceland, and might lead to suspicion of Magnus as another foreign 'expert' adviser.

The second major area of difference between Iceland and the US is firearms. It turns out there are loads of guns in Iceland; you guessed it: the country has the highest per capita gun ownership in the world. But these are entirely for hunting; handguns and assault rifles are banned. Guns are rarely used in crimes, and the police are unarmed. Unlike the police in the US.

Guns are really important to American policemen. The bad guys are heavily armed: the police need guns to protect themselves and their colleagues. To research this series I read a fascinating book called *Into the Kill Zone* by David Klinger, which is a thorough analysis of what happens when American police officers shoot civilians. We have seen in the news examples of this that are unjustified. But many times police use their weapons in legitimate acts of self-defence. In tough areas they are aware that they might come under fire at any moment, or that someone might make a grab for their gun. There is genuine danger, and genuine bravery. Magnus was a homicide detective in the rougher parts of Boston, and so the absence of guns in Iceland would strike him.

Clearly there is a need for the police to have some access to firearms, and so the Icelanders have a specialized unit, a kind of SWAT team called the Special Unit of the National Police Commissioner. They used to be known as 'the Viking Squad', a wonderful name, and in my books they still are. Rural police stations have their own firearms locked in safes; from what I can tell, these are never used on people, just polar bears (see Chapter Sixteen).

Iceland has much of the technical support that is available to advanced police forces. Many of its senior officers have studied abroad. There is a forensics unit based in Reykjavík who will dash off anywhere in the country to a murder scene. They have a computer forensics department, something that is ever more important as phones and laptops contain so much of people's lives. DNA has to be sent for analysis in Norway or Sweden, which can take weeks. There are an increasing number of CCTV cameras throughout Iceland.

One camera I spotted on a trip north intrigues me. About fifty kilometres north of Reykjavík on the Ring Road that circumnavigates the country is a tunnel beneath Hvalfjördur ('Whale Fjord'). As you emerge, a little camera snaps your licence plate. This is about the only route to get from Reykjavík to the north, so it should be possible for the police to check every car that makes that trip. Useful when checking up on suspects.

At first I was careful to note down the various departments within the Reykjavík Metropolitan Police, but they have been reorganized at least twice, and often the names don't translate well into English. Many Icelandic crime writers and their translators use CID, and that's probably the best bet, although I use the now defunct title 'Violent Crimes Unit'. The man in charge of the whole country's police service is the National Police Commissioner, which is a good title.

Rural police organization changes just as rapidly. I have visited a number of police stations around Iceland. At the biggest one in a region, there is normally a chief superintendent, but he or she may have only a dozen officers whose job it is to police a large region encompassing several small towns. If there is a homicide, then they will often call in specialist support from Reykjavík (i.e. Magnus). If a suspect is arrested, they might be taken to the prison at Litla-Hraun. There is therefore a lot of driving involved, but also opportunities for Magnus to range outside Reykjavík to solve his cases.

There are drugs in Iceland: cocaine, amphetamines, ecstasy and marijuana. Lithuanians are often blamed, as are the Dutch and motorcycle gangs. By the way, the largest motorcycle club in the country, which as far as I know isn't involved in drug dealing, is known as 'the Snails', with typical Icelandic irony. The first bank robbery in Iceland didn't occur until 1985; apparently it's difficult to rob banks where everyone knows everyone else.

There have been no serial killers since a Snaefellsnes farmer named Axlar-Björn in the sixteenth century. Icelanders believe their streets are safe; babies are left in pushchairs outside cafés, and young women roam around Reykjavík all night alone. Sadly, a recent murder made some Icelanders rethink this. A young woman named Birna went out for a night on the town one Saturday in January 2017, and didn't come home. She was last seen at 5 a.m. on the streets of Reykjavík. The whole country went looking for her; after a few days someone found her shoes in the lava field near Hafnarfjördur – disturbingly, the same lava field which Pétur had suggested to me many years before would be a good place to hide a body. Eventually her corpse was found washed up on the shore on the south coast of the Reykjanes Peninsula. The police identified two suspects: fishermen from a Greenlandic trawler that had docked in

Hafnarfjördur. They sent a helicopter out to the boat to pick them up.

The nation was shocked. It was one of those tragic times when an innocent place becomes that little bit less innocent.

FAVOURITE PLACES – MOKKA KAFFI

Reykjavík has plenty of good cafés, but my favourite is Mokka. It's a few yards up Skólavördustígur (the Skola Street) on the left, in a building that used to be white but is now raspberry red. It is supposedly the oldest café in Reykjavík, founded in 1958 by an Icelander returning to Reykjavík from Naples where he had been studying music. The warmth and friendliness of the place hits you as soon as you walk in, subtly conveyed by the smell of coffee mixed with waffles and strawberry jam, the house speciality.

It's a small café with leather benches, booths and wood-panelled walls under yellow light. These are hung with pictures by Reykjavík artists that rotate monthly: abstracts, photographs, landscapes, all for sale. Often, the artist will be there too, willing to talk about their work.

The staff are young, friendly and of course speak perfect English. I have often suggested Mokka as a place to meet my sources. It has a reputation as a hangout for artists, writers and intellectuals, a sort of Icelandic Deux Magots, with better waffles.

Reykjavík has many good cafés. Grái Kötturinn ('the

Grey Cat'), on Hverfisgata, is just as cosy as Mokka and famous for its large American-style breakfasts. Babalú, further up Skólavördustígur, is like a little bit of Morocco swept in some Saharan storm to a wet rock in the Atlantic. And Reykjavík Roasters is a classic hipster artisanal coffee place complete with mysterious metal equipment and sacks of coffee scattered around. There are no Starbucks in Reykjavík, but the local chain, Kaffitár, is pretty good: the kind of place where you can linger over a book or a laptop and a cup of coffee.

9 THE SAGAS

My next appointment was with a lecturer in Icelandic Literature, Thorsteinn. I needed to talk to him about sagas. His office was on the top floor of the old building of the University of Iceland. Rather unsettlingly, this reminded me a little of my trip to Berlin to research my 1930s novel: it had a touch of the Nazi Gothic about it. Thorsteinn's office was small and academic, with the exception of an unexplained Barbie doll on the top shelf. Nothing in Iceland is ever completely serious. There was a view over Reykjavík City Airport to Thingholt and the Hallgrímskirkja.

Just in front of the university is a rather elegant statue of an early Icelandic academic, Saemundur the Wise, and a seal. Like many future Icelanders, Saemundur studied abroad, at the Sorbonne in Paris, specializing in the devil and black magic. In the eleventh century, travel from France to Iceland was tricky, so Saemundur did a deal with the devil, who promised to take the form of a seal and give him a lift home. Saemundur hitched the lift, but as soon as he made landfall in Iceland he whacked the seal over the head with a bible. I suppose the moral of that tale is be careful about giving lifts to academics in Iceland, especially if they are carrying bibles.

I mentioned to Thorsteinn that my story was going to involve Tolkien and a lost saga. Back in England, I had read a lot of sagas, and a little about Tolkien. I was not at all surprised to discover that Tolkien was an expert on them and that *The Lord of the Rings* was indeed inspired by one. For my story I needed a lost saga. I had some ideas, but I wanted to check whether they made sense to an expert.

The sagas are a series of stories written down in Iceland in the later Middle Ages in Old Norse. They fall into several categories. There are the lives of the saints, the lives of the Kings of Norway and histories of Europe – there is even a saga about Thomas Becket.

There are a couple of sagas which deal with ancient Germanic myths, including *The Saga of the Volsungs*, which tells the story of a cursed ancient ring, the Andvaranaut, which is passed around various gods, heroes, dwarves and dragons, leaving death and destruction in its wake. The story inspired Richard Wagner's *Ring Cycle*, and of course Tolkien's *The Hobbit*.

The most famous sagas are *The Sagas of the Icelanders*, which are stories about the families that settled Iceland in the ninth to the eleventh centuries. Forty of these survive; some are short, some stretch to a couple of hundred pages. They are not exactly histories, they are more historical novels, even thrillers. They are expertly told, with deft, sparse characterization, plenty of action, legal disputes, wagers, stallion fights, people falling in love with other people's husbands or wives, pride, jealousy, grief. It truly is all there, and in a modern translation they are real page-turners. I love them, although I must admit that some are written better than others, and they could all do with a good editor cutting out chunks of repetition and digression.

The big four are *Njal's Saga*, *Egil's Saga*, *Grettir's Saga* and *The Laxdaela Saga*. My favourite is *Njal's Saga*, which is basically a legal thriller. Njal is an expert lawyer who advises his friends on how to solve disputes at the Althing without resorting to swords and battleaxes. They don't always listen, people die, houses burn. Egil was an extraordinary man and definitely deserves his own saga. He was born in Norway, and from an early age started beating people up unnecessarily. He got kicked out of the country, and went to Iceland, where he settled near Borgarnes on the west coast – his farm still stands at Borg a few kilometres to the west of town. He became a warrior, and fought for the Anglo-Saxon King Athelstan in York. As well as being a thug he was a brilliant poet, and when imprisoned by Athelstan, he wrote a beautiful poem to secure his own release. He returned to Iceland, grew old and a little dotty, and buried his treasure. It has never been found.

The sagas are emphatically not just about men. Some of the best characters are women, such as Gudrun of *The Laxdaela Saga*, who was beautiful, very clever and very dangerous. It was not a good idea to be either her husband or her lover. The women in the sagas are not necessarily the peacemakers: they urge their husbands to get off their fat arses and take revenge against thieving neighbours if they ever want to have sex again.

By the way, these names – Njal, Egil, Grettir, Erik – bring all kinds of difficulties to someone writing in English about both ancient Vikings and modern Icelanders. The conventions are different and inconsistent. I mentioned that Icelandic grammar is a nightmare. Well, even the names need to be declined depending what case they are. The likes of William Morris, being classically trained, decided to lop off the suffixes which give the names their case, and refer to just the root. So Njáll becomes Njal, and our old friend Eiríkr hinn raudi becomes Eirík the Red, which is further anglicized to Erik the Red. However, modern translations of Icelandic always use the full nominative form of the name: Njáll and Eiríkur (Eiríkr is Old Norse). So, in the same book I can refer to a modern Icelander as Egill and the old Viking poet and thug, Egil. Icelanders hate it. Copy editors hate it. I am sure the copy editor of this book will hate it. Sorry. [I do hate it. Suggest change to make consistent throughout *copy ed.*]

If you haven't read the sagas, you might imagine them to be like the Anglo-Saxon poem *Beowulf* or the tales of the court of King Arthur. In fact, they are much more straightforward and down to earth. In the original Old Norse, the language is sparse, the word choice precise, more Hemingway than Proust. Unfortunately, the nineteenth century translations into English by William Morris and Eiríkur Magnússon are quite wordy, and there are quite a few dodgy renditions out there. Magnus Magnusson's translations are much more readable, and the current Penguin translations are excellent. This is a case where it's definitely worth paying for quality; be wary of free, poorly translated editions on the internet.

I was on the hunt for a plausible lost saga. How did it get lost? Whom was it about? Originally, the sagas were written down by monks on vellum (calfskin). They used quills from the left wings of ravens or swans – better for right-handed scribes – and ink made from willow or bearberry. There were hundreds, possibly thousands of copies of the sagas scattered throughout Iceland. By the eighteenth century, an Icelandic scholar who lived in

Denmark named Árni Magnússon became worried that the stories might become lost, and travelled around Iceland for ten years collecting them. Iceland was poor, and he found scraps of vellum containing sagas repurposed for all kinds of everyday uses, such as shoe insoles or the back of a waistcoat. He gathered his collection together in fifty-five boxes, and took them all back to Copenhagen in 1720. He became the librarian at the Royal Library, and stored the sagas there. In 1728, a fire swept through Copenhagen, destroying the library. Árni saved what he could, but many sagas were lost. Which was bad for Norse literature, but good for me.

One of these lost sagas concerned a Norseman named Gaukur (or maybe Gauk? I call him Gaukur, breaking my rule above. Oops). We know it once existed, because there is a gap for it in the Mödruvallabók, with the note 'Insert here the saga of Gaukur Trandilsson'. It was never inserted.

So who was this Gaukur? He is mentioned in a couple of other sagas, as Gaukur of Stöng. According to *Njal's Saga*, he was killed by his own foster-brother, Ásgrímur. Why? I wondered. And where was this place Stöng? I checked it on my map of south-west Iceland and discovered that Stöng was very close to Hekla, the voluble volcano that has erupted many times over the centuries, and which became known as 'the mouth of hell'. Indeed, in 1104 a Hekla eruption completely smothered Gaukur's farm at Stöng, and the valley in which it was situated.

Perfect.

Thorsteinn listened to my outlandish ideas patiently and kindly, and suggested various improvements and modifications. The day after my meeting with Thorsteinn, I drove to Stöng. With some trepidation: Thorsteinn mentioned that he had been scared when he had driven there with his parents when he was twelve.

Stöng is about 120 kilometres to the west of Reykjavík. After leaving the city, you drive up through desolate heath – stones, electricity pylons and steam from the earth bubbling beneath – until you suddenly arrive at the top of an escarpment with a dramatic view of a flood plain, dotted with farms and the odd town, sea and mountains in the distance. Mighty rivers such as the Hvítá and the Thjórsá bring meltwater from several glaciers churning through this plain down to the Atlantic. On the far side of the valley I could see Hekla, with its year-round white crown, a glacier.

I crossed the plain, Hekla growing ever larger, until I came to the River Thjórsá: wide, cold, the white-green colour of melted ice that had once fallen as snow thousands of years ago. As I drove upstream, ever closer to the volcano, the landscape became bleaker, the lava newer, twisted into pinnacles of frozen black trolls, heads of dogs and ravens. The higher I went, the more powerful the river seemed to become, and I wasn't surprised to see pylons striding across the landscape from an unseen hydroelectric dam. There seemed enough force in that water to power the whole of Reykjavík.

I eventually came to a bridge over a narrow gorge through which the Thjórsá squeezed in a churning torrent and, just on the other side, the turn-off to Stöng. A rough track bucked and wove around a rocky cliff down to a partly visible valley of stone. A simple wooden fence bore a sign: '*Lokad*'. Closed. For a moment I considered driving around it – I had come all this way after all. But I resisted the temptation. May is early spring in Iceland. Snow is possible. Many minor roads remain closed until June. Even then it is unwise to drive on them in little cars like my rented Golf;

you really need a four-wheel drive. Driving down that track, sustaining a puncture or a broken axle and walking back to the main road for help would be very stupid. (Sadly, it's the kind of thing tourists in Iceland do all the time.)

Fortunately, higher up the road I could look down on the valley of Stöng, which even nine hundred years after the eruption was a barren moonscape of stone, rock and dust. A thousand years ago, it would have been a lush green valley, with meadows, sheep and a Viking longhouse.

In 1939, archaeologists discovered the site of Gaukur's farm at Stöng, and excavated it. A replica stands just off the main road, a long wooden building with a turf roof that reaches almost to the ground and no windows. Hekla broods close by.

I had found my saga.

Back to London, and time to write the book.

I was looking forward to it, but I was also scared. I'm always nervous when starting a new book. Nobody wants to write a dud, but this one was really important. After the failure of the financial thrillers and the spy novel, this was Plan C. There was as yet no Plan D, and I didn't fancy drawing one up. Plan C had to work.

For encouragement and perhaps a few tips, I read the novels of two British crime writers who had successfully set detective series in foreign countries: Craig Russell and his Fabel series in Hamburg, and David Hewson and his Nic Costa novels in Rome. They were convincing, well plotted with believable characters and, most importantly, authentic settings. They were extremely well written. On the one hand that was encouraging. On the other hand, could I write that well? Welcome to author paranoia. We all have it. It may even be a prerequisite for success; at least that's what I tell myself.

I am a little slow. Publishers like to publish a book a year; I write a book every fifteen months. It breaks down into five months planning and research, five months writing the first draft and five months rewriting and faffing around. The faffing around seems to be an indispensable part of the process.

I had done the research. Writers break down into planners and 'pantsters'; those who like to plan the book in advance and those who write by the seat of their pants, starting with a good idea and seeing where it takes them. Obviously, pantsters are cooler than planners. Stephen King is a pantster. He's also a genius, which is cheating. I am a planner.

I plan the plot and I plan the characters. I like to know where I am going and who is going there before I start writing. I do allow myself to deviate from the plan as I write. That's one of the most enjoyable parts of the process: when you are immersed in writing the story and it suddenly occurs to you that a character might not be exactly who you think he is, or a plot might take an unexpected twist. I usually let it, even though it screws up my plan. I nearly always come up with a better ending just as I am approaching it. My brain cannot seem to conjure up a brilliant idea out of nothing. It needs an existing story structure that works, and then sometimes, just sometimes, something a little better, a little different, will occur to me. I'm not a genius. Pity, that.

Still, I had some good ingredients. I had Magnus. I had Iceland. I had a lost saga about a ring. I had a university professor found dead by the lake at Thingvellir. I could make a story out of that. At this stage I didn't have a title: *Magnus I* would have to do.

Writing *Magnus I* was a lot of fun. I liked Magnus, and it was good to know that we were just getting acquainted; in my previous novels, my heroes, as I naively persist in calling them – protagonist is just too analytical even for me – had come and gone. I hoped Magnus and I would be together for a while. And it was fun to write about Iceland. When the writing is going really well, I feel that I am actually there, on the streets of Reykjavík or the slopes of Mount Hekla.

I had my photographs of Iceland to refer to, and my notes. Lots of notes. I had spent a week cutting and pasting notes from all my reading and my trip into a Word document, sorted under headings like 'Bars', 'Thingvellir', 'Police procedure', 'The Tjörnin'. In the ten years and four novels since *Magnus I*, this document has become massive, over four hundred pages. But it definitely helps when writing a novel. Or even this book.

When writing my eighth financial thriller, I came up with a little trick which works quite well. At the quarter-way stage, I stop and reread what I have written and think about it. Is the book going the way I intended it? If it's not, is that a good or a bad thing? Are the characters developing in an interesting way? And, most importantly, now I am well into the book, do I have any ideas about new directions the plot or characters might take? I usually do. This means I have to go back and make changes to what I have already written, and also to my plan. I do this again at the halfway stage, and before the ending. It takes time, but it strengthens the book, and also cuts down on the rewriting required for second drafts.

There are some writers who don't need editing, who get it right the first time under their own steam. Some of these are overconfident; some of them are geniuses. I am neither of those writers. If there is a problem with a book, I like to know about it before it's published, or, in the case of *Magnus I*, before it even goes out to publishers to accept or reject. I recruited Richenda Todd, an old friend from university who is a professional editor, to help. We embarked on a second draft, polishing style, strengthening characters, improving plot and pace.

I also sent the novel to Pétur, who kindly agreed to read it and point out the errors in my descriptions of Iceland, big and small. Pétur explained that there was no chance of him publishing the book in Icelandic: Icelanders wouldn't see the point of a crime novel set in their country written by a foreigner. Fair enough. And that made me more grateful for his generosity in helping me.

Looking back at them now, he had some useful corrections, such as 'There are no apple trees in Iceland', 'Jaywalking is not illegal in Iceland', '*Anna Karenina* is not available in Iceland' and 'In the sagas it is not so clear who are the good guys and who are the bad guys'.

Carole and I had agreed that her assistant Oli would act as my agent – I would be one of his first clients. But he had to like the book. He read it. He liked it. Together, we came up with a plan. Oli sent the manuscript out.

I was nervous. Extremely nervous.

It takes a while for publishers to respond to submissions, even when supplied by an agent, but I received a couple of quick rejections of the 'not one for us' variety. That's better than the 'this book is a load of old crap' variety.

I tried not to panic. I told myself that if a publisher was going to say yes, they would take their time to get back: the manuscript would have to be shown round to colleagues; sales and marketing would need to be convinced. But, frankly, the waiting was difficult. What the hell would I do if they all said 'no'? There was no Plan D.

They didn't all say no. We found a publisher, Corvus, a brand-new imprint set up by Atlantic Books with Nic

Cheetham in charge. Nic was young, imaginative and enthusiastic (he is still the latter two if not so much the former). He was setting up this completely new imprint, and he was excited. Kindle was just beginning to take off, and Nic saw it as an opportunity for smaller, nimbler publishers, rather than a threat. His enthusiasm, and that of Oli, fired me up. Publishing was fun again.

Magnus I was not a great title, and so I had submitted the manuscript under the title *Fire and Ice*. Nic had a better idea: *Where the Shadows Lie,* a reference to the verses in the epigraph of *Lord of the Rings*. That was a good title.

Where the Shadows Lie was published in March 2010. Someone, I don't know whether it was Nic or a hidden person I had unwittingly met in Iceland, organized the most spectacular publicity stunt. In April of that year Eyjafjallajökull erupted, spewing ash into the atmosphere all over the northern hemisphere, stranding air travellers and placing Iceland firmly on the map. The book did reasonably well in physical form, but thanks to Nic's efforts the ebook sold extremely well, getting to number one.

Oli swung into action. He managed to sell the novel to fifteen publishers throughout Europe and the United States, mostly on the back of the *Lord of the Rings* angle. This was very gratifying. But the best news came from the smallest country. Pétur wanted to publish the book in Icelandic.

Phew! No Plan D. Time to write *Magnus II*.

There are two ways to get to the Blue Lagoon from Reykjavík – the Blue Lagoon is the large geothermal pool-spa next to a power station, and is well worth visiting, although it is expensive. One way is to take the main highway to the airport and turn left on a well-paved road following the tourist buses.

The other way is by the back roads, turning off the main road just past Hafnarfjördur and following signs to Krýsuvík. The small road passes Seltún, a geothermal area of vents, mud pots, hot springs and sulphurous ponds that simmer and burp amid hillsides of red, yellow and orange, and water of an other-worldly green-blue. Just south of these is the 'draining lake', Kleifarvatn, which sprang a leak in its floor in 2000, revealing a hundred metres of black volcanic sand and rock around the shore. All around here, you are very aware that something in the ground beneath you is unsettled. The place is spooky, especially when the mist moves in.

Even spookier is Selatangar. When you reach the coast, head west towards the fishing village of Grindavík, which is near the Blue Lagoon. Just before the town, keep your eyes out for a turn off to the left to the car park for Selatangar.

At first Selatangar looks like nothing more than a typical Icelandic lava field of rocks, rubble and twisted black stone, some of which tumbles into the sea. As you walk to the east, threading your way through the rock on a narrow footpath, the rubble begins to take on form. There is a man-made breakwater, and then the contours of black circular walls take shape from the surrounding stone. As you come closer you realize that these are dwellings, or former dwellings. For centuries – from the Middle Ages until the 1880s – men used to come here to fish for a few months every spring. Spring in Iceland is a season of storms and occasional snow. It is hard to imagine a place more bleak or inhospitable than these black rock booths blending into the black lavascape.

Yet the place has an ethereal, lonely beauty. On one side the sea ripples and rages, on the other, steep mountain slopes rise, and in between the lava field guards the ghosts of those fishermen. I visited on a day when snow streaked the lava, and fog curled in from the sea to smother the ruined huts. Eider ducks bobbed in the current just a few yards offshore. Driftwood lined the black stone beach – bleached wood from trees that had once grown in Canada or Siberia. There was no green to be seen anywhere.

One ghost in particular survives, Tanga-Tómas, who has been seen in the area many times. At Selatangar it's hard *not* to believe in ghosts.

11 BUST

While I had been writing *Where the Shadows Lie*, happily losing myself in thoughts of sagas, rings, volcanoes and Gull beer, the financial world was melting down around me.

I remembered how I had explained to the German author ten years before that it would never be possible to write a financial thriller set in Iceland, and now the country was smack in the middle of the biggest financial crisis the world has yet seen. Friends urged me to write another financial thriller. I was reluctant.

But I couldn't ignore it. Especially since I had resolved to write about issues that went beyond Iceland. As a foreigner I wanted to write about Iceland's interaction with the outside world, about big issues, not small ones, and there was no bigger issue as far as Iceland was concerned than the financial crash. It was a subject that I knew well, and the intersection of greed, hubris, ambition and self-delusion in the people who caused it was exactly the kind of thing I had examined in my financial thrillers. Yet I felt I needed to place distance between my new books and my old. It had been hard enough to make the leap from one to the other and I was glad I had done it. Writing about the perpetrators of the crisis seemed a step backwards.

But what about the victims? *That* interested me much more. Especially since the response by ordinary Icelanders was more immediate and more effective than anywhere else in the world. They began their 'pots-and-pans' revolution and it worked. They overthrew their government.

The financial crash slammed into Iceland hard. With hindsight, Iceland may not be the country that suffered most, that honour probably falls to Greece, but the Icelanders suffered first.

Icelanders call the depression after the financial crash the *kreppa*, which also means 'pinch'. The financial crisis was started by people throughout the world figuring out clever new ways of getting around stodgy restrictions to borrow too much money. I say clever, but these schemes turned out to be profoundly stupid. What was true globally was also true in Iceland.

As the *Iceland Review* said in 2009, 'The crash is the fault of thirty men and three women. All these people are connected.' In the early 2000s a new breed of young entrepreneur emerged in Iceland. They were called the *útrásarvíkingar*: *útrás* is the opposite of invasion, so this literally means something like 'outvading Vikings'. Let's call them 'the Outvaders'. They were in their thirties and forties, they were ambitious, quick-thinking, decisive and bold. They built successful companies from very little: supermarkets, insurance companies, food manufacturers, bottlers, fund managers. And banks. They invested in high-profile businesses overseas, especially in London: West Ham, Hamleys, Mothercare, House of Fraser, Oasis, Karen

Millen. And banks. And they did it all with borrowed money.

They had fun. Unlike their low-key predecessors, the old 'Octopus' families of import-exporters, they flaunted their wealth. One of the most prominent of these Outvaders was Jón Ásgeir Jóhannesson, the owner of the Bónus supermarket chain, who supposedly amassed debts of $8 billion by the time everything fell apart. He owned a distinctive black private jet that was seen flying in and out of Reykjavík City Airport regularly. He hung out in the bar of London's trendy Sanderson Hotel. His wife founded Reykjavík's trendiest hotel, 101. He owned a superyacht in Miami called *The Three Vikings*, and a ten-foot statue of a Viking with a Fender Stratocaster electric guitar strapped to his back stood proud in his London office. This kind of consumption was matched or exceeded by hedge fund managers, investment bankers and Russian oligarchs, but for a country as small as Iceland, with its history of poverty and egalitarianism, it was remarkable. Where had all that money come from so quickly?

Iceland's banks grew in parallel with its businessmen. There were three of them: Landsbanki, Glitnir and Kaupthing. In the 1990s Kaupthing's capital was only a couple of million dollars. In the 2000s it bought banks throughout Europe, including the venerable merchant bank Singer and Friedlander in London. In 2007 it set up an internet bank, Kaupthing Edge, which took deposits throughout Europe. Within a year the bank had pulled in £2.5 billion of deposits from 160,000 customers in the UK alone. Landsbanki set up a similar internet bank called Icesave in 2006, which operated mostly in the UK and Holland, and within two years it had amassed £4 billion of deposits in the UK.

The global financial crisis didn't start in Iceland. Bankers in the US found clever ways of lending too much money to mortgage borrowers who couldn't repay it, and passing these risks on to banks throughout the world. No one could quite work out how many of these bad mortgages there were, and who ultimately held the risk. The banks didn't trust each other. When Lehman Brothers, an American investment bank, could no longer borrow to fund its activities, it went bust. Now nobody trusted any bank. For a few days in October 2008 it looked as if the ATMs in Britain and America would stop working.

And in Iceland. The Icelandic banks were reliant on the goodwill of foreigners, and this was no longer forthcoming. They didn't have the funds to repay international depositors who were becoming nervous. Every Icelander knows where they were on the afternoon of 6 October 2008 when Prime Minister Geir H. Haarde addressed the nation. Clearly shaken, he sowed panic among his fellow citizens. He closed the speech with the ominous words: 'God bless Iceland.' The banks were nationalized.

Doubt immediately fell on Kaupthing Edge and Icesave, the two Icelandic internet banks operating in London. Alistair Darling, the British Chancellor of the Exchequer, announced support for British banks, including British-based subsidiaries of foreign banks, like Kaupthing Edge. But Icesave, as a branch not a subsidiary of Landsbanki, was technically the responsibility of the Icelandic government, who didn't seem to be willing or able to guarantee their deposits. So at 10 a.m. on 8 October 2008, Alistair Darling announced that he was freezing the assets of Icesave. Ten minutes later, it was done. The only method Darling could employ to justify this legally was to invoke the Anti-Terrorism Act of 2001.

This was a stretch, but Darling believed that if ordinary depositors in the UK lost money in any bank, there would be a run on all the banks and the whole economic system of the country would collapse. Mr Darling saved the British financial system. Just. But he screwed Iceland, or so the Icelanders believed.

The Icelandic currency, the króna, collapsed. Many Icelanders lost all their savings. The country itself was close to bankruptcy: the British government demanded three billion euros to compensate it for repaying Icesave's British depositors. Like everyone else, many Icelanders had borrowed too much, but the financial fiddlers had come up with a particularly pernicious instrument of self-harm in Iceland: the foreign-currency mortgage. House buyers had borrowed in yen or Swiss francs at low interest rates. When the króna collapsed, the amount these borrowers owed tripled in local currency. There was no chance they could ever repay their loans.

Icelanders were furious. They were furious with the Outvaders. They were furious with the bankers. They were furious with Prime Minister Geir Haarde, and the previous prime minister and current governor of the Central Bank, Davíd Oddsson, and they were particularly furious that as a country they all owed Britain and Holland over three billion euros as a result of the activities of an internet bank they hadn't even heard of. Being called a bunch of terrorists by Alistair Darling didn't please them either.

So they took to the streets, or rather the square. Every Saturday, throughout that winter, protesters gathered in the square in front of Parliament to protest, banging pots and pans to make a noise. Icelanders famous and not so famous spoke, singers sang, signs were waved, protests were chanted. It's dark for most of the day in Iceland in winter:

people carried torches and lit fires to warm themselves. The crowds grew from 2,000 to 7,000. There was some violence. Food was thrown: mustard, tomato ketchup, eggs and skyr. The police made some arrests and occasionally used pepper spray and tear gas. As I have already described, flagstones were thrown and two policemen went to hospital.

But, on 26 January 2009, Geir Haarde resigned. The revolution had been a success, and a relatively peaceful one at that.

Throughout the world, people wanted to lock up those bankers who were responsible for the crash. Iceland is one of the few countries that actually managed to do it.

It started with a public discussion on the TV show *Silfur Egils*, the name of which refers to our thuggish poet friend Egil from the sagas and his lost silver, but is presented by the journalist Egill Helgason. One of his guests, Eva Joly, was a Norwegian-French judge who had some bracing suggestions for bringing the perps to justice. She was persuaded to spend several months in Iceland advising the government.

There was a strong suspicion among many that the Outvaders, the bankers, the politicians and indeed the lawyers of Reykjavík all knew each other too well, and so the government searched for a prosecutor from outside the capital to go after the culprits. They found one in the small town of Akranes, Ólafur Hauksson. This all seemed a bit of a joke at first. Ólafur had no experience of financial crime: the only picture of him I could find on the internet was of a comfortable middle-aged man with an enormous grin standing next to a river holding a very large salmon. Which was kind of apposite, since you may remember the Icelandic phrase for 'Big Cheese' is 'Big Salmon'. Anyway, Ólafur got himself a small office in Reykjavík, a couple of computers and three colleagues, and set to work going through documents. Methodically. Unlike other countries' prosecutors, who imprisoned the small fry and fined the companies, Ólafur built up his team and kept going until he found the bosses responsible. He didn't let the shareholders of the banks pay the fines, as happened in Britain and the US; he was going after people, not institutions. And it worked. Senior executives at all three of Iceland's banks were successfully prosecuted. They went to jail.

So where did all that money come from? How did Kaupthing go from capital of a couple of million dollars in the 1990s to deposits of many billions? In London, the gossip was that the money came from Russia. I checked this out. While it was true that one of the Outvaders had cashed out from successful bottling and brewing investments in St Petersburg, which may have inspired the rumour, I could find no evidence of Russian oligarchs' money sloshing around the Icelandic banking system.

Once again, the culprit was 'clever' ways of borrowing. Banks are allowed to borrow several times their capital. So a bank with capital of £1 million may have made loans of £10 million, back before the crash. What if £1 million of those loans was made to someone to invest £1 million of new equity in the bank? Then the bank would have £2 million of capital and be able to lend £20 million. £2 million is lent to someone to invest in the bank, which now has £4 million of capital. And so on.

Sounds clever, doesn't it? Money is magicked out of money. The Icelandic bankers thought it was clever. That's how they had so much money to lend, to themselves and to their Outvader friends. It's not actually that clever, it breaches many regulations, regulations that the bankers either didn't know about or thought were just red tape. These men are not nearly as crooked as many of the financiers I have come across during my career in the City where I invested in junk bonds, or when writing my financial thrillers, men like the people who put together fake mortgages and sold them on or, more importantly, the people who managed these men. My impression, which is backed up by the views of bankers in London who dealt with them, is that the Icelandic bankers were optimistic, naive and lacked judgement rather than evil masterminds. Don't get me wrong: they broke rules that were put there for a reason, they should have been punished and they have been.

The Independent Party was thrown out of government. Jóhanna Sigurdardóttir became prime minister, the first openly lesbian leader of a country. The comedian Jón Gnarr stood for mayor of Reykjavík in 2009. He is well known as the lugubrious manager of a petrol station in the sitcom *The Night Shift*. He stood on a manifesto of a drug-free Parliament by 2020, a polar bear for the zoo, tollbooths at the border with Seltjarnarnes and the construction of a large white-collar prison for foreign bankster criminals. His motivation for becoming mayor was it would be nice to have a chauffeur to chat to while he was driving to work. He won, but, like many politicians before him, he didn't keep his promises. There is no polar bear in Reykjavík's tiny zoo – probably a good thing too.

Eventually, after several years of pain, Iceland has pulled itself back on to its feet. Tourism, which has been booming for several years now, saved the economy. The 'For Rent' signs have disappeared in Laugavegur, the skyline is dotted with cranes again, and brand-new Range Rovers –

which had become known by locals as 'Game Overs' – are once again seen powering down Reykjavík's roads. But there remain people who are having difficulty paying the mortgages they took out in 2006. The fallout from the *kreppa* still overshadows many ordinary Icelanders' lives.

12 CHARACTERS

What if a group of ordinary Icelanders, angry Icelanders, met at one of these protests in the Parliament Square? What if they decided that those responsible for the crash deserved to be punished? Directly. By them.

That was my idea for *Magnus II*.

I decided my ordinary Icelanders would be a fisherman, a middle-ranking bank executive, a writer, a student and a junior chef. Now I needed to find something out about these people.

I have developed a useful technique for exploring my characters. First I locate someone similar to the character in question, usually the contact of a contact, and arrange to meet them. I don't know why, but in my experience almost everyone wants to meet an author writing a book about people like them. I don't ask extremely personal, direct questions. I tell them about my character, what he or she is like, their parents, their fears, their ambitions, where they live, what car they drive. I then ask them what's wrong with my description. At this stage there is always something wrong and they are eager to tell me. Next I ask how I can improve the character. We work on it together. It's fun. They tell me about the ambitions the character would have, their habits, their doubts, their bugbears, their inner conflicts. Of course, often they are projecting their own deeper feelings, but sometimes they are talking about their friends or their family. The character comes alive.

Let's take the fisherman. My initial idea was that his name was Björn. He was in his early thirties, tough, from a family of fishermen, and came from Sandgerdi, a fishing village near Keflavík Airport at the south-western tip of Iceland. He had borrowed to buy a boat in foreign currency, and suddenly, after the *kreppa*, he had no chance of paying back his loan.

To discuss Björn, I met Linda at Kaffitár in the middle of Reykjavík. Linda described herself with a smile as a 'quota princess'. This is because her father is a 'quota king'. To understand fishing in Iceland you have to understand fishing quotas. To understand Björn, I needed to know his quota situation.

OK – I know fishing quotas sound dull, but this bit is genuinely more interesting than you might expect, so don't skip it.

Fishermen are Iceland's heroes. This wasn't always the case. Although there have always been millions of fish swimming around Iceland, it was a nation of farmers. Only in the early twentieth century, with the invention of the outboard motor, did Icelanders started catching fish in a big way themselves, from small inshore fishing boats. As the century progressed, Iceland pushed the limits of its fishing waters further and further offshore. Herring became a massive source of wealth in the 1960s, as well as the ubiquitous cod. Fishermen were tough, independent, courageous and, during the herring boom, rich. The chain of small fishing villages that surround the rim of Iceland became prosperous.

As the catches grew, the fish stocks dwindled and, like fishing nations everywhere, Iceland had a problem. Their solution was to implement a quota policy. In 1984, all the fishermen in Iceland were given for free a quota, based on their catches over the previous two or three years. This quota allowed them to catch a certain proportion of the total allowable catch set by the fishing ministry every year. These quotas could be traded.

In many ways this new system worked brilliantly. The authorities enforced total catches that were low enough to ensure that fish stocks recovered, and Iceland's fisheries became sustainable. The owners of larger boats were able to buy up the quotas of their smaller colleagues, making fishing much more efficient. Iceland's economy prospered and fishing remains one of its key export industries.

But it was undeniably unfair. It was a windfall for a small proportion of Iceland's population. Fishing captains grew very rich. They became quota kings. They bought expensive houses in Seltjarnarnes. A group of them banded together to buy Stoke City football club in England. And while the owners of the boats did well, there were fewer fishermen on bigger fishing boats, and so employment in the industry fell. It was tough for the smaller operators, like my character Björn.

Despite its success economically, and the much-needed foreign currency it earned after the *kreppa*, fishing remains a divisive issue in Iceland. Some people think the quotas should be taken back by the government. The fishermen themselves tend to support the conservative Independent Party, and to oppose joining the European Union; they don't want Brussels messing with their fish.

Linda took me down to the harbour and I met her father. At first sight he didn't look particularly big, or tough; in fact, he seemed mild-mannered, polite and friendly. But he had huge hands, and a face etched with a thousand wrinkles through which bright blue eyes twinkled. Linda had explained how he was a canny businessman, but when I asked him how my character Björn could become a successful fisherman, he said he would learn to think like a cod. And he would love to fish. He would have started fishing as a boy and never have been able to give up.

By the end of meeting Linda and her father, I knew all about Björn and his boat and his problems.

Then I met Birna, a middle executive in one of the banks, who had lost all of her savings in the bank's money market fund, and then her job. In London I met Kristján, an Icelandic graduate student. Pétur told me about Icelandic writers. I was getting to know my characters.

Now we come back to the thorny issue of stereotypes. In the first draft of my very first financial thriller, I included a character who was the 'muscle' working for an American businessman. I called him Luigi, gave him thick dark hair and an overcoat. As one of my friends said, he was a cliché. So it's all very well figuring out what a typical Icelandic fisherman, or student, or banker is like, but sometimes you need to make them different from the typical.

An example is Hákon, a rural priest in *Where the Shadows Lie*. I found myself an Icelandic priest, a woman named Sara, and she gave me a portrait of a typical cleric living in the countryside. He would be big, bearded, an amateur scholar, conservative, old-fashioned, possibly with responsibility for working the farm attached to his church. He would be interested in the devil, and be willing to wield the appropriate prayers to get rid of him. Apparently the devil is big in Lutheran theology, and fear of the devil is certainly a part of rural superstition.

The Reverend Sara and I discussed what atypical interests or hobbies the priest might have that would nevertheless make sense. We decided he liked heavy metal, especially Led Zeppelin. In the book, Hákon sits in his isolated vicarage by his lonely church in the dale at Hruni and cranks up 'The Battle of Evermore' to full volume. It works for me.

For me, my most interesting recurring character is Vigdís. She is Magnus's sidekick, a detective in the Reykjavík Violent Crimes Unit. Sidekicks are common in detective fiction, from Sherlock Holmes's friend Dr Watson onwards. They perform a useful function in a story: they are a foil for the detective to test out theories, they create conflict, they provide a different perspective, and they are an ingredient in possible subplots.

I wanted to make Vigdís a little different. I decided to make her the opposite of the classic image of a young Icelandic woman. I decided to make her black.

When I suggested this to Icelanders, they explained that there were very few female detectives in Iceland, and that there was no chance that there could ever be a black one. I took that as a challenge: I would invent one. Vigdís.

There are not many black people in Iceland. Some are recent immigrants: unlikely for a police officer. Some were adopted – that was possible. But I decided it would be more interesting if Vigdís was the daughter of a black US serviceman at the Keflavík air base, and an Icelandic woman who worked there. That idea I liked.

I have never witnessed any racism in Iceland, and indeed the English-language journalism in the country is uniformly tolerant and encouraging of ethnic diversity. But a number of Icelanders have told me that some of their compatriots can be racist. This might be expected in a society as homogenous and isolated as Iceland's. I remember working on a farm in Norway when I was eighteen and being surprised by the attitude of the very kind farmer's wife towards black people . She had just never met one before. During the Second World War, the Icelandic Prime Minister Hermann Jónsson requested that the Americans refrain from sending any black servicemen to their air base at Keflavík, a prohibition that persisted until 1972.

Vigdís never met her father, and so was brought up by her mother – her last name, Audardóttir, references her mother Audur rather than her father. Her mother is an alcoholic, a depressingly common problem in Iceland. Vigdís has dark skin, but rather than embracing her blackness, she chooses to deny it. Strangers speak to her in English, assuming she is a foreigner, but she refuses to answer in that language. In fact, she refuses to speak it at all. She sees herself as an Icelander through and through, but her compatriots don't always agree. The ambiguous attitude that she has to her Icelandic identity is something she and Magnus have in common. Her race causes her difficulties; I like difficulties in a novel.

I have identified a couple of mixed-race Icelanders with whom I could discuss Vigdís. Together we could talk about her character, change it, make Vigdís more like them. But I'm not going to do that. To me, Vigdís is a real character, and I'm not going to let anyone mess with her. Apart from me. Sometimes you just have to use your imagination.

13 SNAEFELLSNES

I wrote my story about my demonstrators in the Parliament Square, and their plans to take justice into their own hands. I called it *66 Degrees North*, which is the latitude upon which Iceland sits. It's also the name of an Icelandic clothing company – I checked and they were quite happy to have their brand as the title of the book. Unfortunately, my US publishers decided that Americans wouldn't understand the concept of latitude, and so the book is called *Far North* in America. This is inconvenient for everyone: in an age of social media which transcends boundaries, I live in fear that some of my American readers will buy the same book twice. And, as far as I can tell, Americans *do* understand the concept of latitude.

I sent the book to Nic, my editor at Corvus. He liked the story. But he said it should include some of the myth and superstition that infused my first book, *Where the Shadows Lie*. Very occasionally editors try to make you do things that make no sense to you. Sometimes you need to be persuaded. More often they are clearly absolutely right. This was one of those times.

There were three possibilities to add myth and/or superstition: ghosts, elves or the sagas. I wasn't yet confident in my ability to handle ghosts or elves – that would come later – but I loved the sagas. So I needed a saga.

And a subplot. I had referred to the death of Magnus's father when he was twenty in America. Perhaps it had something to do with his family back in Iceland – the grandfather's farm where Magnus had stayed when he was a boy? I could create all kinds of flashbacks and conflicts in a farm somewhere in rural Iceland. Yes, I needed a farm.

I had another look at *Iceland Saga* by Magnus Magnusson, and came upon the story of the Berserkjahraun, or 'Berserkers' Lava Field' told in *The Saga of the People of Eyri*, otherwise known as the *Eyrbyggja Saga*. I've always been intrigued by berserkers, those Scandinavian warriors who would drive themselves into a frenzy – go berserk – in the middle of a battle and kill everybody around them, so I read the saga for myself.

Eyri refers to Snaefellsnes, the peninsula that juts out to the west of Iceland about 120 kilometres due north of Reykjavík as the raven flies. At the tip of this peninsula rises Snaefellsjökull, the volcano in the shape of a perfect cone which you can sometimes see from the capital.

The Berserkjahraun is a lava field that flows in an immense river of stone from the mountains that form the spine of Snaefellsnes to the sea on its northern shore. In the saga, there were two farms on either side of the lava field: Bjarnarhöfn, meaning Bjorn's harbour, and Hraun, meaning lava field. Bjorn, the son of Ketil Flat-Nose and brother of Aud of the deep mind, was the original settler at Bjarnarhöfn. A hundred years later, Vermund the Lean lived at Bjarnarhöfn and his brother Styr lived at Hraun.

There was only a couple of kilometres between them, but the lava field was impassable.

Vermund went raiding and trading in Norway and returned with a gift from the King of Sweden: two berserkers. When he arrived back at Bjarnarhöfn, he found the berserkers too much trouble to control, and gave them to his brother Styr at Hraun. They worked hard, but one of them fancied Styr's daughter and wanted to marry her. Since the berserker had no money to pay for her, Styr said he could only marry his daughter if the berserkers cut a path through the lava field.

The berserkers set to work furiously, and eventually cut the path. They were exhausted. Styr suggested that they rest in his new sauna, which they did. Styr poured water through the skylight of the sauna, which became so hot the berserkers rushed out, whereupon Styr ran them through with a spear.

I liked that story. Maybe Magnus's grandfather could have a farm by the Berserkjahraun, at Bjarnarhöfn perhaps? I could start the book with the grandfather, whose name was Hallgrímur, playing berserkers in the lava field as a child in the 1930s.

I needed to check this place out. I jumped on a flight to Iceland, hired a car, and drove north. I passed by Reykjavík and turned on to the Ring Road. This is Iceland's main road, and it is well maintained. It circumnavigates the island, a distance of about 1,300 kilometres. I haven't yet driven the whole distance, but I am determined to do it one day.

North from Reykjavík the road ducks through the tunnel under deep Hvalfjördur, then emerges and follows

the fjord inland for a few kilometres, rounding a mountain
on the inland side, and then emerging on one of the most
windswept stretches of road in Iceland. The road is raised,
and follows a curve with the sea and the flat islands of
Borgarfjördur on one side and a high smooth-sloped fell on
the other. Gusts of wind are so strong here that cars can be
blown off the road. I kept both hands tight on the wheel,
and although I could feel the car being buffeted, I made it
over the long low bridge that crosses the road to Borgarnes,
the main town in the western region.

Just north of Borgarnes, the road forks, and I turned left
along a stretch of empty highway, passing the warrior-poet
Egil's farmstead at Borg. On one side, in the distance, I
could see the whitecaps of the sea. On the other a high wall
of green and grey mountain, a curtain of stone through
which the clouds danced, sometimes white and ethereal,
sometimes black and threatening. Rain showers came and
went, speeding in from the sea, occasionally followed by
strips of sunshine and spectacular rainbows. Time to crank
up Beethoven's Fifth on the car's CD.

Rivers tumbled down in waterfalls from the mountains,
hurrying underneath the road towards the coast, water
skipping over rocky ledges and pausing for respite in deep
clear pools. I passed occasional farms, each with its lush
green home meadow, and horses standing hopefully in the
fields. What they were hoping for I was not quite sure.

A volcano had spewed its molten guts here several
thousand years ago, and left walls of frozen stone, nibbled
by green and orange moss. A bump appeared in the
distance, and grew: a flat rim like an upturned saucer –
Eldborg, the dormant crater that had presumably created all
this mess.

The road veered to the left just past the crater, and

ventured out on to Snaefellsnes. I could see the south shore of the peninsula and the bottom of the volcano, but it and the ridge of mountains that runs along the spine of the peninsula were shrouded in cloud.

At Vegamót, a name on a map that just means 'Where the roads meet' and consists of barely more than three buildings, I turned right and climbed a valley cut into the flank of this mountain ridge. This is known as the Kerlingin Pass after the Kerlingin troll. She used to creep down from the mountain at night to steal babies from the local town of Stykkishólmur. Trolls have to get back to their cave by daybreak, but one morning she was too late, and became frozen in stone. You can see her up above the old pass which runs parallel to the road, a column of rock with a sack of babies over her shoulder, but at that moment she was covered in cloud.

The valley became increasingly narrow as the road rose ever higher, a stream rushing down beside it. Sheep looked up and ran across the road in front of me, timing their foray perfectly so I had to brake. Ewes were followed by lambs as big or bigger than them, desperate for an udder. It was damp, lonely and a great place for a chase at the end of a book.

I was in the cloud now, driving slowly. I rounded a sharp bend, and the road began to descend. In a minute or so I emerged from the cloud into bright blue sky, and a view that blew me away. In front of me was Breidafjördur, or 'Broad Fjord', with its countless islands. Closer by were extraordinary hills, piles of rock and metal that had been created by volcanic activity, hundreds of feet high. Their flanks were brown and grey, but also yellow and red, orange and green as the various metals infused in their fabric had oxidized. Beneath these hills tumbled a sea of stone, waves of frozen lava a hundred feet high marching down to the sea. A single red hut cowered beneath the rock, perched on the edge of a winding lake created by the lava flow several thousand years ago.

And there, along the seashore, stood just two farms, the same farms that had stood there a thousand years ago when Vermund the Lean and his brother Styr inhabited them: Bjarnarhöfn and Hraun.

The lava field was, of course, the Berserkjahraun.

I drove through the Berserkjahraun to Bjarnarhöfn.

I had tentatively decided that this would be Hallgrímur's farm. I could have invented a farm; perhaps I should have done. Bad things happen in my books at Bjarnarhöfn, and real farmers live there and have lived there in the past. But I much prefer to write about a real place. It's not just for the sake of the book; it is for my sake when I am writing it. Bjarnarhöfn is seared into my brain; when I am writing a scene set there, I feel that I am actually at that beautiful spot by the fjord.

And it is a beautiful spot.

It is a large working farm cut off from the rest of Snaefellsnes by mountain, sea and lava. To the east is the Berserkjahraun lava field, to the south a massive, steep mountain rears up, and to the north and west lies the fjord. A tiny wooden chapel stands in a meadow between the farm buildings and the sea. This church was built in 1856 and is little more than a one-roomed hut, but it contains a seventeenth-century altarpiece and a thirteenth-century chalice, both gifts from grateful shipwreck survivors. The cove just to the west of the farm is known as Cumberland's Bay after the English merchants from Cumberland who used to visit there in the Middle Ages.

One of the farm buildings has been converted into a shark museum, stuffed with the old paraphernalia of Icelandic fishermen, but the highlight is the rotten shark, or *hákarl*. This is an Icelandic delicacy. Greenland shark is buried for a few weeks and then hung in drying racks in the next-door shed to rot. Eaten raw, or cooked immediately, the meat of this shark is toxic. But left to rot, or rather ferment, it is just about edible. It smells strongly of ammonia, and when you first taste it, it blows out your sinuses. It is best eaten on a toothpick with a chaser of *brennivín*, an Icelandic schnapps-like spirit that will definitely blow out your sinuses if the shark doesn't get them first. Some people really like it; some don't. It is Iceland's answer to Marmite. You have been warned.

From the farm, one can look east over the sea of lava to the Kerlingin troll with the babies on her back, atop her mountain, and a lonely bump in the plain between the mountains and the fjord. This is Helgafell, or 'Holy Hill'. It was deemed holy by one of the first settlers in the area, Thorolf Most Beard, who believed his family would enter it after their death and forbade anyone from doing their elf-frighteners on the hill – 'doing your elf-frighteners' is the polite Viking term for defecating.

In the churchyard at its foot is the grave of Gudrun Osvifursdottir, Iceland's first nun, and the heroine of *The Laxdaela Saga*. You will remember she was involved in a bloody love triangle, and her enigmatic last words in the saga are inscribed on a rock at the foot of the hill: 'To him I was worst whom I loved best.' If you walk from her grave to the ruined chapel at the top of the hill, in silence and with a pure heart, then your wish will be granted. I climbed the hill, but near the top I slipped, fell and swore, so my wish wasn't granted. But I promise I didn't frighten any elves.

Helgafell is a few miles south of the pretty town of Stykkishólmur, the largest community on the peninsula. A natural harbour is formed by a seabird-strewn island at the mouth of a cove. The harbour is full of fishing boats and a ferry to the West Fjords, on the other side of Breidafjördur. I dropped in at the local police station to talk to the region's chief constable and the deputy magistrate, and then went to meet Ásta, an Icelander living in Surrey, who spends her summers in Stykkishólmur working in a hotel there. She told me a little about her childhood in the town. She was terrified of the Kerlingin troll. Until recently much of the town was owned by a Franciscan convent, including the regional hospital of St Francis, which is the biggest building in town. Ásta remembered the French and Belgian nuns, who spoke poor Icelandic, conducting their services in Latin with incense; they seemed to Ásta incredibly exotic. I wondered how Stykkishólmur had seemed to the Belgian nuns.

Ásta's father was from a family of twelve who had grown up on one of the islands in the fjord. There are lots of these, especially just offshore from Stykkishólmur. Apparently there are two things you cannot count: the stars in the sky and the islands in Breidafjördur. They have tried, of course. They have counted more than three thousand islands at high tide, but if you include the rocks and skerries that emerge at low tide, the number is indeed unknown. You won't be surprised to hear how all these islands were created. The Kerlingin troll got angry one night, and she threw three rocks at the people of Stykkishólmur. They missed, but shattered into countless pieces.

This tiny little town is home to one of Iceland's most extraordinary modern churches. The style is space-age Mexican. Smooth and white, it boasts a sweeping tower with three bells at the top, a smooth nave and a bubble apse at the back. The bell tower and the apse reminded me of churches in New Mexico; the rest of the building recalled science fiction films from the 1960s.

Further out along the peninsula's north coast I passed through the fishing villages of Grundarfjördur and Ólafsvík. Just outside Grundarfjördur is one of the most photographed mountains in Iceland, Kirkjufell or 'Church Fell'. This is a tower of rock and moss that overlooks a calm lagoon. The shifting light and shadow from the low sunlight at this latitude, the constantly changing clouds and even the Northern Lights, illuminate the rock and the moss of the mountain in a shimmering palette of different colours, all of which are reflected in the water beneath it. It is easy to take a great photograph here, and every one is different.

Ólafsvík used to be the port for Greenland, and a few miles west of the town stands the church of Ingjaldshóll. A local story claims that an Italian nobleman came to stay with the priest there many centuries ago. Christopher Columbus recounted in a letter to Queen Isabella that he had once sailed to Iceland on a Bristol merchant ship, and spent a winter there in 1477, fifteen years before he discovered America. When I first heard that it got me thinking: surely there is a book in that somewhere? It took me seven years to find it: *The Wanderer*.

From Ólafsvík I drove back over the mountain spine of Snaefellsnes. This route was even more remote and desolate than the Kerlingin Pass. I was actually climbing the foothills of the Snaefellsjökull, but it was only when I had descended to the south coast that I could see the mountain properly.

It is an almost perfect conical volcano topped by a glacier. Almost perfect because there seems to be a small stone thorn, which looks a bit like a question mark, that emerges from the summit. Much of the time, you can't see the top. Clouds love Snaefellsjökull. Billowing white clouds foam over the summit; angry black clouds gather and brood. Often, one white cloud hovers over the glacier formed from the warming ice in an otherwise blue sky, while the sunlight strokes the ice in yellow, turning to pink as the afternoon fades.

I have never made it to the top. Apparently, from the summit on a clear day, you can sometimes see the massive white ice cap of Greenland, shimmering upside down just above the horizon, in the polar mirage known to Norwegians as an *is-blikk*.

It is a special place. Jules Verne came to Iceland and was bewitched. This is the entrance for the *Journey to the Centre of the Earth.* In more modern times New Age mystics have flocked to the area. Ley lines spread out from the mountain like a star. Arnarstapi, the little town at the foot of the mountain, is a mystic melange of elves, trolls, gnomes, candles and incense. One blue wooden cottage even has a Tao emblem on its wall. It's all just a little much. However, there is a good walk a couple of kilometres along the black cliffs to the neighbouring village of Hellnar.

Just to the west of Hellnar is the site of the farm where Gudrid the Wanderer was born in about 970. She was born in Iceland, got married in Greenland, had a child in America, returned to Iceland and then travelled to Rome. All in about the year 1000. The farm is now just a meadow with a rather graceful statue of Gudrun and her son Snorri.

Sitting there, looking out over the Atlantic, I thought to myself: wouldn't she make a good book? Another ingredient for what eventually became *The Wanderer*, published many years later. It is extraordinary how long it can take an idea for a book to take shape.

FAVOURITE PLACES - THE BERSERKJAGATA

The Berserkjagata is signposted, but it's hard to locate. As you descend from the pass, you turn left on the main road from Stykkishólmur to Grundarfjördur, the D54, and after a short distance turn right, following a sign to Bjarnarhöfn. After about a kilometre driving through the Berserkjahraun, the road forks. You take the right fork and park on the road just at the edge of the lava field, where the road comes closest to the shore. Look out for a tiny wooden signpost to the Berserkjagata, but even now it is hard to find. Walk across the grass to the lava and you will find a narrow path cut into the rock. This is the Berserkjagata, the 'Berserkers' Street', a path from Hraun to Bjarnarhöfn cut through the rocks by the two berserkers a thousand years ago.

Follow it. In a few moments, you will find yourself out of sight of the road, alone in a sea of stone. By now you will be familiar with Iceland's lava fields, but this is a great one to walk through. The lava rears up in agonized, twisted shapes. The path rises and plunges with the rock. Moss, lichens and berries nibble away at the stone in colours that are both surreal and beautiful: lime green, orange and bright yellow; and in autumn the leaves of the berries flame red.

This walk is at its most atmospheric on a day of mist and moisture, when clouds overwhelm the mountains to the south, and tendrils of mist creep up from the fjord, slinking through the stone towers. This is the point where the lava poured into the sea, creating quiet coves where cormorants and eider ducks paddle, watched by the occasional sea eagle, and the only sound is the water lapping gently at the foot of the stone river.

As you pick your way through the lava field, you eventually come to a depression, which forms a small natural amphitheatre. Just to the right of the path are some raised stones, too flat and square to be natural. They look like a large grave. In the nineteenth century, these stones were excavated, and underneath were found two unusually large skeletons.

How cool is that?

14 ELVES, HIDDEN PEOPLE AND GHOSTS

I had written two full-length novels set in Iceland, and it was becoming clear that there was a question I could no longer dodge. What was I going to do about the elves?

I have related how I first heard about them, from Helga at that dinner during my book tour to Reykjavík. Naturally, I was intrigued, and when I met Icelanders in London during my initial research, I would casually ask them about the elves, or the 'hidden people' as they are often known.

They always took my question seriously. One woman told me that her name had been chosen by a hidden woman, who had whispered it to her grandmother when she was born. You can see from the preceding chapters that elves, ghosts and trolls are important in Iceland, even today. My editor was keen that I should include superstition and myth in my books. So I needed to write about elves.

And yet. I'm not the kind of guy who believes in elves. I write about a tough Boston homicide cop: could Magnus really believe in elves? There are no elves in Raymond Chandler's books, nor in Agatha Christie or even Ian Rankin. And what about the elf-deniers? These are modern, sophisticated Icelanders who resent the stereotype that their countrymen are gullible hicks who believe in fairies. They claim that those who say they believe in elves are just lying. There is a lot of elf-related tourist tat in Reykjavík gift shops, and while I have never attended the famous elf school, it does sound a little like a tourist trap to me. So I was nervous: was the whole country winding me up about elves? I wouldn't put it past them.

But I couldn't write about Iceland honestly and avoid the subject entirely. It was a problem.

Back in London, I made an appointment to see Gudjón, a senior diplomat at the Icelandic embassy, and his colleague Ágústa. They were both helpful, informative and down-to-earth. So, at the end of my meeting, I asked them how I should deal with elves. We had a useful discussion. It turned out Gudjón had an Uncle Gísli who used to play with elves as a child – his mother saw him skipping around with them. Afterwards, Gudjón sent me an article about construction problems in the remote town of Bolungarvík.

It was a classic Icelandic elf story. The government was building a tunnel to provide better all-weather access to Bolungarvík, which is stuck at the very north-western edge of Iceland. The tunnel went through a mountain that was known to be the home of hidden people. Two of the diggers mysteriously broke down. And then, while blasting in a local quarry, there was an accident, and large boulders destroyed some local properties. No one was hurt, but the contractor was naturally concerned, as were the town's residents, many of whom were sure that the incidents were perpetrated by the hidden people angry at the destruction of their home.

The contractor decided to approach locals to help him sort the problem out with the hidden people. The mayor and the town council wanted nothing to do with it, but the priest agreed to say a prayer, and local 'seers' undertook to discuss the matter with the hidden people. Which they did, asking their forgiveness and putting on a small concert for their enjoyment. The tunnel was completed without mishap.

My mind started turning. What if there had been a landslide in Bolungarvík and people had actually been killed? In that case, some people might accuse the hidden people of being murderers. And what if Magnus's boss sent him all the way to Bolungarvík to solve the crime, knowing how frustrating he would find it? Perfect. Thanks to Gudjón, I had my elf story. It's a novella of about sixty pages, and it's called *Edge of Nowhere*.

Who are these elves (*álfar*), or hidden people (*huldufólk*)? First, we need to pin down whether there is a difference between the two. Some Icelanders insist that there is, and that to conflate the two is to show ignorance. But the more you dig the more confusing it becomes. Everyone is sure what a hidden person is, but less clear about elves, if they are not in fact hidden people. Terry Gunnell, Professor of Folklore at the University of Iceland, believes that the confusion comes from the fusion of two parallel sources of the myths: Norse and Irish folk tales.

Hidden people are a lot like other Icelanders. They lead parallel lives, unseen most of the time. They are wary of humans, but willing to help out if need be. They will provide advice if necessary; they will rescue travellers in distress. They can be charming, and there are several cases recorded of shepherd girls going up to the mountains to look after their sheep and being seduced by hidden men. Strangely enough, the resulting babies are always visible; the 'hidden' gene must be recessive.

Most farms have a family of hidden people living on or near their property, usually in a prominent rock. This knowledge is passed down through the generations, and locals will be careful not to disturb the hidden people's dwelling. Hence the Bolungarvík story. And the famous story of a road near Álftanes, just outside Reykjavík, whose route was slightly changed to avoid dynamiting a rock where elves were known to live. This story is highly contentious: the elf-deniers claim that it was distorted by journalists trying to hype up a non-story.

Many Icelanders do take elf dwellings seriously. The Icelandic author, Yrsa, is also a civil engineer. She writes:

> My personal encounters with elves are few, only one to be exact. This was in 1997 and occurred while I was supervising a new pipeline being placed in Mosfellsbaer, a suburb of Reykjavík. The contractor doing the work mentioned in a progress meeting that his equipment kept breaking down while attempting to remove a large boulder smack in the middle of the pipeline's planned route. He believed this to be the result of elves, that they were sabotaging his equipment to protect their home. This was noted in the minutes of the meeting and the project owner, Reykjavík Energy, needed no further prompting – the pipeline layout was altered to avoid the rock. The equipment worked fine after that.

Do Icelanders believe in elves? A small minority certainly do. Most people's grandmothers do. Some people don't, don't think any of their countrymen do either and are profoundly irritated by foreigners asking them about the subject. In my experience, many, perhaps most, Icelanders keep an open mind. They know that the laws of science suggest that hidden people are unlikely to exist. But they are part of Iceland's society and culture, and of that traditional way of life and world view which in a couple of short generations is in danger of being lost. Many Icelanders not only regret that loss, but respect the way that their grandparents lived in a kind of harmony with their landscape. It's something they want to hold on to.

I heard Ed Miliband, former leader of the British Labour Party, interviewing Katrín Jakobsdóttir, Iceland's prime minister, on his podcast *Reasons to be Cheerful*. After a serious discussion on gender inequality in Iceland, he asked her about the elves. You could hear the panic in her voice. What should she do – deny an important part of Icelandic culture or admit to believing in the hidden people? For a second she seemed to be taking the elf-deniers' side. But then the seasoned politician took over and she pivoted to trolls, explaining how trolls must be stupid because they always seem to be caught out by the sunrise and turned to stone. Miliband pointed out she had probably lost the troll vote, but in fact she had deftly avoided the elf wars.

The Icelandic countryside teems with folk stories. Every village or even farm has one, and they don't just concern elves. We have heard about the trolls, but there are also sea monsters, seals, serpents, polar bears and sorcerers, as well as assorted goody-goody pastors and saints.

There are also ghosts and 'seers'.

Most towns still have their seers, or fortune tellers, and many people will explain that one of their extended family has the gift. The country is also teeming with ghosts. In general, these are more benign than British ghosts. Like the hidden people, they will offer helpful advice rather than scare the living daylights out of you. One Icelander told me how a relative was able to communicate with her dead grandmother, who occasionally warned her of impending disaster. This relative was reluctant to admit her ability to anyone; she wasn't an attention-seeker, and it raised all kinds of problems – what should she do with the information her grandmother gave her? Wouldn't people think she was crazy if she told them she had been speaking to ghosts? So she kept quiet.

She became a character in *Sea of Stone*, a farmer's wife, Aníta, who learns unsettling things during the book that she is unwilling to pass on. In England I don't believe in ghosts, and I wouldn't dream of writing about a character speaking to the dead. But in Iceland? It almost seems wrong not to. There is something about the country, the light, the shadows, the landscape, the rock, the myths, the desolation that makes you feel that the supernatural is natural.

Every other year, in November, a crime-fiction festival known as Iceland Noir takes place in Reykjavík. In 2018, a group of about twenty delegates drove up to Snaefellsnes and the lovely Hótel Búdir. After dinner, we repaired to the cosy bar, a lava field and a small, isolated church lurking in the darkness outside. Yrsa suggested that we tell each other ghost stories.

The Icelanders had some great ones, well told, and a couple of the Americans present put in a good performance. The British less so. We are uncomfortable with ghosts. But, as an English rationalist, I felt the odd one out; the one who didn't get what was obviously all around me.

After half a dozen stories, the hotel receptionist asked if we wanted to hear about the hotel's ghost. We did. Her name is Pálína and she was a chambermaid at the hotel for many years; her grave is in the graveyard beside the church. She loved the hotel and she was conscientious. She still is.

Staff there have become used to her tidying up late at night; the receptionist recounted several examples. This can be inconvenient. The way the staff persuade her to withdraw and let them get on with things is a simple 'Thank you, Pálína', which usually works.

So, if you do come across a ghost in Iceland, be polite.

FAVOURITE PLACES – HÓTEL BÚDIR

The Hótel Búdir is my favourite place in Iceland.

It stands next to its black church alone, halfway along the south coast of Snaefellsnes. It is a spectacular location. To the north rises the wall of mountains that runs along the spine of the peninsula, spouting long white streams of waterfalls. To the east, a golden beach stretches for several kilometres along which horses gallop beside the blue waters of Faxaflói Bay. To the south the Black Church perches on a low ridge. Looking to the west, you gaze over a treacherous lava field surrounding a raised crater, and beyond that the breathtaking Snaefellsjökull.

The hotel bar is cosy, with a telescope to examine local eagles. The food is excellent – lamb, fish, seafood, samphire – and the dining room faces west towards the volcano. Sunset takes its time in Iceland, and you can spend the whole meal watching the light on Snaefellsjökull turn from yellow to pink to red, until finally, once the sun has disappeared beneath the horizon, it gives the glacier an ethereal yellow halo. Room 6 contains a desk with a great view of the glacier. Halldór Laxness, Iceland's most celebrated novelist, used to stay here; I fantasize about spending three months in that room writing a book. Because it is so isolated, Búdir gets very dark at night, and the hotel is a fine place from which to see the Northern Lights. If you ask, the hotel staff will give your room a call if the aurora does its stuff in the middle of the night.

The Black Church stands on a low hill two hundred metres or so from the hotel. The church is small, painted black, with a white door and windows. A little graveyard surrounds the church, enclosed by a wall of neat black lava stone topped with turf, and at its entrance stands a traditional white Icelandic-style lych-gate. It has become a popular venue for weddings, with the Snaefellsjökull the perfect backdrop to a wedding photo. If you walk – carefully – through the lava field to the south of the church for about ten minutes, you will find the ruins of the village which it served, once the main trading station for the whole peninsula. This lava field is treacherous, dotted with caves and crevasses, one of which supposedly leads to a jewel-encrusted tunnel that goes all the way to Reykholt, many miles inland. Unsurprisingly, the place is teeming with elves.

15 VOLCANOES

One evening in April 2010 I was on my way to an event in a library in Chiswick in West London to talk about *Where the Shadows Lie*, which had just been published. I was a little early, so I wandered through a park, running over the talk in my head. I was at that awkward moment in the book cycle where I had three books in my head: the book I was promoting (*Where the Shadows Lie*), the book I was writing (*66 Degrees North*) and the book I was going to write next (?, *Magnus III?*, *Help!*). I was searching for a topic for the next one. Like *The Lord of the Rings* and the financial crash, I wanted it to be something relevant to Iceland, but also of worldwide importance.

My phone rang. It was my wife, Barbara. She was in Beijing and had just been told that her flight back to Britain was cancelled because of a volcano in Iceland. This was the beginning of a fraught week for Barbara, who, after a few days hanging around in Beijing, returned to London via New York, Madrid, Saint-Malo and Portsmouth. But it was good news for me: I had the subject for my next book.

Every volcanic cloud has a silver lining.

Eyjafjallajökull.

The first thing to do was learn how to say it. This is not as impossible as it first seems. There are two things you need to know. The first is that Eyjafjallajökull is made up of three words: *eyja* ('island'), *fjalla* ('fell' or 'mountain') and *jökull* ('glacier'). The second is that 'll' is pronounced 'dl'. So Eyjafjallajökull becomes eh-ya-fyadla-yerkudl. Kind of. If you say that you will be close, and let's face it, with most Icelandic words 'close' is as near as you are ever going to get.

The next thing I needed to do was to set up 'Ejz' as Eyjafjallajökull in Autocorrect in Word, so that I could type the word Eyjafjallajökull easily as often as I needed to. It's still there, in Autocorrect. Eyjafjallajökull. See?

I needed to get over to Iceland to find out more. It was a few months after the eruption by the time I arrived there, but the signs of the destruction were still visible. Dust devils of ash whipped up in the wind beneath the volcano, and the bridge over the nearby river was being reconstructed.

I visited the local police station at Hvolsvöllur and heard all about it. They had been busy.

The eruption had happened in two stages. The first was at a place called Fimmvörduháls, which lies between Eyjafjallajökull and the neighbouring glacier of Mýrdal. This was a pretty event. A line of craters spewed lava up in the air, glowing orange, red and yellow against the white ice of the glacier. A sludge of molten lava oozed down from the craters. People flocked to see it, arriving by snowmobile, super-jeep or helicopter. The police's main job was to prevent tourists from doing stupid things, like sticking their toe in the lava to see if it was really hot (it was). But nobody died.

Then came the big one. Eyjafjallajökull itself is a broad ridge under an ice cap. It's often in cloud, and it was when the main eruption happened. There were rumbles, there were earthquakes, there were explosions, but you couldn't see anything. And then the jökulhlaup came – literally 'glacier run'. When a volcano erupts under a glacier, ice melts quickly. A lot of ice, very quickly. The water tumbled down the north side of the mountain taking boulders and earth with it, destroying everything in its path. Eyjafjallajökull is a few kilometres inland from the southern shore of Iceland, on the eastern edge of the fertile plain I described earlier. The jökulhlaup stormed around the mountain and overwhelmed the Markarfljót river, dragging down bridges in its headlong rush to the sea.

Local construction workers were diverted to the bridge of the main Ring Road over the river, and there are some amazing pictures of a brave lone digger-driver desperately creating holes in the road around a long low bridge to allow the waters to pass as the jökulhlaup approaches. Another more direct jökulhlaup leaped down the southern slope almost taking out a farm.

The clouds cleared to reveal a continuing eruption throwing ash thousands of feet into the air. Or at least that's what it looked like from a distance. Near the volcano, the sky had turned black, as if day had been turned into night. The heavier ash particles fell on farmland, covering grass and crops with a thick grey film containing metals poisonous to animals. The farmers herded their livestock into barns and kept them there. Amazingly, nobody died.

The finer ash particles rose higher into the atmosphere and drifted south-west over Northern Europe. Little bits of Icelandic volcano fell on the roof of my car outside my house in London. Much more importantly, flights were cancelled amidst fears that the particles would destroy aero engines. People were stranded all over the world, including Barbara.

By coincidence, Wikileaks was in Reykjavík at the time, editing the video of an attack on Iraqis which had just been leaked to them.

So I had the subject for my third Magnus novel, *Meltwater*. A group of hackers are editing a video in Reykjavík and they take an afternoon off to go to see a volcanic eruption. One of their number is murdered next to the volcano. None of the suspects can leave the country.

There have been about thirty volcanoes active in Iceland since the Norse settlers arrived. The island was created only twenty million years ago. It stands on the Mid-Atlantic Ridge, a chain of mostly underwater mountains created by volcanic activity as the European and North American continental plates rip apart from each other. In Iceland, the volcanoes reach the surface, where they simmer, bubble and occasionally explode.

Let me introduce you to some of them.

We have already met Snaefellsjökull, the prettiest of them all with its almost perfect cone and its topping of ice, that hovers above Snaefellsnes. It is taking a nap at the moment – the last time it erupted was about AD 200.

We have also met the most active, Hekla. This is sited just to the north of Eyjafjallajökull, and can be clearly seen from sixty miles away. It is nearly classically volcano-shaped – a cone with hunched shoulders – but the summit is actually a line of craters covered in snow and ice. The mountain looms over the surrounding landscape, and the closer you get to it, the more evidence you see of its past temper tantrums: devastated valleys and ramparts of frozen lava. It has erupted many times recently, in 1947, 1970, 1980, 1981, 1991 and 2000. Most adult inhabitants of

Reykjavík will have driven out to watch it at some time. Nothing since 2000. Hmm.

There were some truly massive eruptions in the early Middle Ages, all the more noticeable because Hekla is close to some of the most fertile land in Iceland. We saw how Stöng was smothered in 1104 in a surprise eruption that was talked about throughout Europe; Cistercian monks claimed that Hekla was the gateway to hell. In the eruption of 1341, flocks of birds were seen flying into the volcano, which onlookers assumed to be men's souls. With good reason, Icelanders were scared of it. No one dared climb it, until two brave students reached the summit in 1750. It is possible to climb it today – about three and a half hours from the car park – but it involves walking on snow past sulphurous craters.

Not far from Hekla, and very close to Eyjafjallajökull, is Katla. This volcano slumbers unseen beneath the beautiful Mýrdal glacier. Since the settlement of Iceland, it has been one of the most active volcanoes in Iceland, but we haven't heard a peep from it since 1918. It's bigger than Eyjafjallajökull, and more destructive. This is because of the jökulhlaups associated with it, flash floods that periodically trash the land to its south. The police station I visited had numerous evacuation plans for when or if Katla erupts: it often erupts soon after Eyjafjallajökull. I visited a farmer near Hella who was worried about an eruption, and had made plans. There is a reason why all the farms in that part of Iceland are situated on small hillocks.

But you only really understand the devastation caused by Katla when you drive east along the coast, past the village of Vík. Just out of town the landscape becomes what can only be described as desert. Mile upon mile of sand, empty of all habitation, just the modern Ring Road, which will probably be washed away in the next eruption. There is a fascinating fishing museum in Vík, and a monument to the fishermen of Hull. The debris from Katla stretches out to sea, and makes the waters treacherous for ships. Over the centuries there have been hundreds of wrecks, many of fishing vessels from Hull. Tragically, many shipwreck survivors died when they walked along the uninhabited shoreline searching for a village, when they should have headed inland towards the hills.

As you fly towards Iceland from Europe, or as you drive along the Ring Road from Reykjavík to Vík, you see a group of cubic islands, which look like poker dice tossed into the sea by some gambling troll. These are the Westman Islands, and they contain two volcanoes of note. One is the island of Surtsey, which is the westernmost die. This thrust itself out of the sea to form an island in 1963 in a spectacular eruption that lasted four years. The island covered one square mile right after the eruption finished, but has already halved in size with erosion. Scientists are trying to keep the island pristine to study how life takes hold on a brand-new chunk of land, but according to the *Christian Science Monitor* an 'improperly handled human defecation event' resulted in a tomato sprouting on the island. It has been removed.

The other volcano takes up half of the biggest Westman Island, Heimaey. The other half is taken up by quite a large fishing port, with a population of about five thousand people – big by Iceland's standards. There are also a *lot* of puffins on the island.

In the middle of one night in January 1973, the volcano erupted. The side of the mountain was blown away and lava started oozing down towards the town. Fortunately, forecast bad weather meant that the fishing fleet of seventy vessels was still in port. With an extraordinary display of speed, initiative and courage, the Westman Islanders evacuated the inhabitants and the sheep as the lava flow reached the town. Of 1,350 homes on the island, about 400 were swallowed up, creating a northern Pompeii. Two unfortunate sixteen-year-olds were in bed with each other, unknown to their parents, but they escaped. Having taken out part of the town, the lava threatened to block up the harbour, which would destroy Heimaey's future viability as a fishing port. Local fishermen managed to stop the lava by spraying it with cold seawater, freezing it halfway across the mouth of the harbour. It worked: Heimaey now has a very useful breakwater, and remains one of the busiest commercial fishing ports in Iceland.

The town survived, the inhabitants returned and only one man died: an alcoholic who tried to break into an abandoned pharmacy. There is a wonderful museum in the town explaining the event. And thousands of puffins still inhabit the cliffs.

But the most devastating eruption of all was Laki in 1783. Laki is another one of those volcanoes that you can't really see because it is hiding beneath an ice cap, this time Vatnajökull, Iceland's biggest glacier, in the south-east of the country.

The eruption took place in the spring. One hundred and thirty-five craters opened up, throwing molten rock three thousand feet into the air. Lava leaked out everywhere. One powerful flow headed for the village of Kirkjubaejarklaustur, a tongue-twisting village of nineteen letters situated on the foothills above the flood plain desert to the east of Vík. (Those of you who counted the letters to check should remember 'æ' is one letter in Icelandic). As the lava reached the village one Sunday, the parishioners gathered in the church, and the pastor, Jón, gave a sermon which stopped the flow. The lava field, two hundred years old now, is of course still very much visible on the edges of the community, not far from the church. Somehow the name of the village, at nineteen letters the longest in Iceland, remained intact.

The lava fires went on for eight months. But the effects of Laki were felt far beyond Kirkjubaejarklaustur, or even Iceland. The volcano tossed huge amounts of sulphur dioxide into the atmosphere, as well as ash containing all kinds of poisonous elements. A blue haze cloaked Iceland; pastures were poisoned. This ushered in the 'Haze Famine'. First the animals died – three-quarters of the livestock in Iceland. Then the people. Iceland nearly failed: there were discussions of evacuating the whole population of the country, 38,000 people, to Denmark.

The haze drifted across Europe, reaching Bergen, Prague, Berlin, Paris and Britain, creating a thick fog and turning the sun blood red. An estimated 20,000 Britons died that summer. Temperatures soared: the summer of 1783 was the hottest on record in Northern Europe, causing thunderstorms that produced hailstones so big they killed cows. Then winter came – 28 days of continuous frost in southern England, and a further 8,000 deaths. In North America, the winter of 1784 was the longest and one of the coldest on record: the Chesapeake Bay froze for weeks, and there were even ice floes in the Gulf of Mexico. The eruption and the crop failures following it have been cited as one of the causes of the French Revolution.

Scary. We've seen what Eyjafjallajökull can do to twenty-first-century life; another Laki eruption would be much worse. But easier to spell.

FAVOURITE PLACES –
JÖKULSÁRLÓN

If you travel all the way to Iceland, you want to see some ice. And the best place to do this is Jökulsárlón, literally 'Glacier River Lagoon', an astoundingly beautiful lake of icebergs in the far south-east of the country.

It's a long way from Reykjavík, nearly four hundred kilometres along the Ring Road on the south coast, past the Westman Islands, past Hekla and Eyjafjallajökull, past Vík, and on the other side of that great flood-plain desert. The lagoon is at the foot of a tongue of the massive Vatnajökull glacier that reaches down towards the sea. It tumbles in extreme slow motion into the lagoon, as large icebergs calve and then drift through the mouth of the lagoon to the Atlantic.

There are tours; there are tourists. But the thing to do is escape them, walk back along the road from the main car park, climb over the high bank and scramble down to the shore of the lagoon. Wear warm clothes, arrange for the sun to be out – not quite sure how you do this – and just sit and watch and listen.

The lake is a bright blue and is crammed with icebergs

of all shapes and sizes. They are white, grey, green and in some places blue with varying degrees of translucence, and they drift imperceptibly towards the mouth of the lagoon. Every now and then a loud crack echoes across the water as ice melts, and in the distance, over the mound behind you, you hear the crash of surf on the nearby shore. But as you sit, you listen to a gentle song of tinkling and dripping. The water is completely still: black with a blue sheen. I caught sight of a fish slithering between icebergs. Behind the lagoon, the tongue of ice rears high up towards the largest glacier in Europe. Stay. Let your mind wander in one of most soothing, peaceful places on earth.

The ice squeezes through a channel to the sea, where waves crash on to a beach strewn with sweating icebergs, and wetsuited windsurfers navigate around the blocks of ice. It's tempting to try to climb on to one of the chunks of floating ice – yet another dumb thing tourists sometimes do in Iceland.

It's a long way to Jökulsárlón, but it's worth it.

16 WILDLIFE – POLAR BEARS AND BIRDS

In November 2016, I travelled to Saudárkrókur, in the north of Iceland, researching my book *The Wanderer*. As is my habit, I dropped into the local police station to speak to the chief constable. On his wall I couldn't help noticing a photograph of a polar bear charging down a hill.

The bear had arrived on Iceland's shores eight years earlier. It had first been spotted by a farmer's daughter, who was in the sheep shed when she heard her dog barking and running across a field towards a bear, which was busy eating eider ducks' eggs. The dog was rescued, the alarm was raised and all hell broke loose. Vets from Denmark were summoned with tranquillizer guns and a cage, but the bear was hungry and it was dangerous.

And no one could see it. The weather had turned foggy, and a hungry predator was on the loose. People from all over Iceland drove towards Saudárkrókur to see the bear. It was spotted by a main road, and a crowd of fifty to sixty people gathered to watch. The local police carefully approached a hill, behind which they believed the bear was lurking. But not carefully enough: whereas the police thought they were stalking the bear, actually the bear was stalking them. The bear charged down the hill towards the crowd of onlookers, and the police shot it.

The bear always gets shot.

At irregular intervals, bears show up on Iceland's shores. They are swept out to sea from Greenland on ice floes, and when they are in sight of land, they swim ashore. They are tired and they are hungry and occasionally they are accompanied by a cub. Polar bears are dangerous at the best of times; in these circumstances they are very dangerous. They end up getting shot, usually by the local policeman. The town museums of Bolungarvík on the north-west coast, and Húsavík in the north, contain stuffed polar bears, shot soon after they came ashore.

Bears have been coming to Iceland in this way for centuries. The first was spotted in 890, sixteen years after Ingólfur arrived on the island, by a farmer in Vatnsdalur.

According to a local folk tale, a helpful polar bear once drifted near to the island of Grímsey, which is just off the north coast of Iceland, bang on the Arctic Circle.

One day all the fires went out on the island. It was in the days before matches, and so three islanders had to cross to the mainland to bring back embers to rekindle them. The sea was iced up, so they had to walk across the ice. One of the men got lost and drifted out to sea on an ice floe.

The next morning, the man was cold and hungry and thirsty, but he was still a long way from land. His ice floe drifted towards another chunk of ice, on which there was a mother polar bear trapped with her cubs. The man was scared, but there was nothing he could do to steer his ice away from the bears. Soon they collided. But the mother polar bear didn't eat the man: she allowed him to suckle her milk with her cubs and kept him warm. When the man had regained his strength, she swam over to the mainland with him on her back. He gathered some embers and then returned on her back to Grímsey, and all the fires on the island could be rekindled. The man was so grateful, he gave the bear cow's milk and two slaughtered sheep, and the bear swam off back to her cubs.

People like polar bears. Many people don't like the police shooting them. In Canada and Alaska shooting polar bears is forbidden. Some say it should be possible to keep a helicopter, a cage and a tranquillizer gun on alert to sedate the invading bears and take them back to Greenland. This is not as easy as it sounds, partly because of the tendency of fearless Icelanders to run around the countryside looking for a bear every time one is seen. The chief of police at Saudárkrókur genuinely regretted having to shoot the bear, but in a number of accounts of polar-bear killings it seems clear to me that the guy pulling the trigger was excited by it, even if he didn't admit it. I can imagine the thrill of the chase, big-game hunting with a real purpose, namely to protect local citizens. And I can imagine the outrage afterwards. People get *really* upset about this. Possibly upset enough to kill?

The idea for my novella *The Polar Bear Killing* was born.

When you are describing a landscape, as I have said, it is important to describe *movement*. Things that move bring a scene alive. And the things that move most obviously in Iceland are birds.

These aren't birds that sit quietly waiting to be ticked off birdwatchers' lists. These are birds that *do* things.

I sometimes think that the ravens own Iceland and

humans are allowed to live there only with their permission. Remember, it was a raven that led Flóki to Iceland in the ninth century. There are loads of them in Iceland. Huge birds that look much like crows, but often act like eagles, they are extremely intelligent. They usually operate in pairs, exclaiming in their distinctive loud croak that can sound like human speech, although ravens produce a wide range of other cries. They seem to be watching you, whether they are soaring high above, or skipping between stones and fence posts. They circle over corpses, of birds, of sheep or of people.

This being Iceland, there are of course plenty of folk tales about ravens. Odin kept two ravens, Hugin and Munin, who served as scouts for him, flying off to gather intelligence. Ravens predict death or weather changes; one even led a girl away from a landslide. Some grandmothers can converse with them.

I mentioned that when I visited Saudárkrókur it was November. There was snow on the ground. The police station is in Church Square, and the whole time I was there, two ravens circled and croaked, often perching on the church tower. They owned the town. I had to put them in the book.

I always show the first draft of my books to an Icelander to weed out the mistakes, and I gave *The Wanderer* to the author Lilja. The book takes place in August, and Lilja told me that ravens only come into town in the winter when they were hungry. It would be very strange to see them in town in August, but if they were there, the local inhabitants would believe that they were foretelling a death. Which was perfect. This being one of my books, the ravens were pretty much correct.

The most common bird in Iceland is the puffin, which

looks like a cross between a penguin and a parrot, but can both fly and swim. The Icelandic word for them is *lundi*, but they also go by the rather lovely nickname *prófastur*, which means 'provost' or 'dean'. They live in burrows, often on cliff faces, in large communities. They arrive in Iceland to nest in April or May. Puffin is frequently found on the menu in Icelandic restaurants – it's tasty if cooked well. One of the largest colonies in Iceland is on the Westman Island of Heimaey. In August the eggs hatch, and the baby puffins, known as pufflings, waddle forth. These are extremely cute: grey and fluffy and a little clueless. They often get lost and wander into town, but teams of local children are allowed to stay up late in the evening and rescue them. The children take the chicks home for the night. The following morning they find a spot near the sea and throw them high in the air. The pufflings glide down to the water and swim off. You have to put some effort into the throw, apparently, or the pufflings won't catch the breeze and will splat into the ground.

I most often associate swans with St James's Park, or perhaps the River Thames, gliding peacefully in sedate surroundings. In Iceland, you can suddenly happen upon small lakes surrounded by lava, in which up to twenty swans paddle. God knows what they are doing there.

Many Icelanders' favourite bird is the golden plover. People eagerly listen out for its distinctive and persistent 'peep', which means that the plovers have arrived in Iceland and spring is here. It is a fine bird, with a royal coat of gold, black and white, and it lurks in the heather.

The word 'eiderdown' comes from the down of the eider duck. The males are black and white and the females dun-coloured. They spend the winter at sea, and then nest close to the shore, often on a farmer's property. They pluck down from their breasts and leave it out to dry, before lining their nests with it to keep their chicks warm. For centuries, eider down was an important source of income for Icelandic farmers, who would watch over nests to keep gulls and ravens away.

There are so many spectacular birds in Iceland, all of them doing something: soaring white-tailed eagles, darting gyrfalcons, dive-bombing arctic terns, paddling harlequin ducks, black cormorants splaying their wings, gannets and fulmars diving into the sea, skuas mugging other birds for food, great northern divers or 'loons' gliding over lakes with their eerie cry, ptarmigans strutting their stuff in the heather, geese formation-flying in the evening sky.

All right, I can't deny it: and chickens, or *kjúklingar*, as they are rather charmingly known in Iceland. Clucking in ugly metal Eimskip shipping containers in farmyards.

FAVOURITE PLACES – THE BEACH AND CLIFFS NEAR VÍK

Vík is a pleasant little town crammed between the beautiful glacier of Mýrdal and the sea, at the southernmost point in Iceland halfway along the south coast. It has no harbour, just a long stretch of black beach. To the east lies the Mýrdalssandur, the sandy desert created by Katla's jökulhlaups. Spectacular cliffs rear up to the west, alongside beaches and dramatic rock formations. It's well worth exploring these.

You can see the rock formations from Vík: a line of tall rock spires just offshore, one of which is purported to be a petrified ship grabbed by a troll (of course).

You can get closer to these stacks, driving out of town and inland around the headland to the black Reynisfjara beach. On one side of the beach a cluster of basalt columns rise like a giant church organ on cliffs crowded at nesting season with birds: kittiwakes, fulmars and puffins. Out to sea, the extraordinary rock formations slosh through the waves as if approaching the land from the Atlantic. And to the west, the spectacular rock arch of Dyrhólaey, Iceland's southernmost point, juts out into the ocean.

This beach is notoriously dangerous. Medium-sized waves wash against the black sand, and it is tempting to go within a few yards of them to look at the sea and the rocks, even to dip a toe in the water. Don't. Seriously, don't. The currents and the undertow are very strong here. But most deceptive are the 'sneaker waves', larger waves that very occasionally stretch up the shoreline to suck away the loose sand under the feet of people who are too close. Tourists die here: by my count of the press reports, two died in 2015, two in 2016, one in 2017 and one in 2018.

If you drive back to the Ring Road, go west a few kilometres and then turn off again, you cross a causeway and reach the top of the cliffs of Dyrhólaey. The views from here are truly spectacular: of the basalt columns and the offshore rocks, but also of the outstandingly beautiful Mýrdal glacier to the north – thick white cream flowing between mountains. And to the east you can see right along the southern shore of Iceland. Birds nest here, including puffins, which means it's possible that the cliffs are closed during nesting season (I didn't notice any closure when I visited in May at 9 p.m., but perhaps I just missed a sign).

The weather in Iceland is terrible. But then it changes.

I mentioned in the last chapter my trip to Saudárkrókur. It was November and it was snowing hard in Reykjavík. I only had four days to get to Saudárkrókur and back, a distance of about three hundred kilometres there and three hundred kilometres back, and I was worried. According to the government website, road travel was not recommended. You don't argue with Icelanders on the subject of snow: if they say it's too bad to drive, it's too bad to drive.

I lost a day, spent in the snow in Reykjavík. The following morning, at about 10 a.m., the website advice changed to a go. So I went.

The first hundred kilometres along the Ring Road were fine. I passed the windy headland by Borgarnes successfully, and drove north through the snow. Then the road climbed to the notorious Holtavörduheidi, the highlands between the west and the north of Iceland. People lost their way and died trying to cross this on foot or horseback well into the twentieth century, and the weather hasn't improved since then. Sure enough, I entered cloud and never left it for another hundred kilometres. I drove along at thirty kilometres an hour, both hands on the wheel, staring hard at the road ahead.

There are beautiful lakes and mountains on either side of the road here. So I am told. I didn't see them. But the snowfall had eased off, the road had been cleared, and I made it to Saudárkrókur.

I didn't have much time. I visited Glaumbaer in the snow. Glaumbaer is where Gudrid the Wanderer lived after she returned to Iceland from Greenland, and it was where a body was going to be found on page one of my next book, *The Wanderer*. In August, without snow, when it would look decidedly different. I then visited the local police, I saw the two ravens circling, and stayed the night at the Tindastóll, one of the oldest hotels in Iceland. And yes, a discussion with the chambermaid confirmed that there was a ghost in that hotel too.

I wanted to give myself plenty of time for the trip back to Keflavík to catch my flight, and so I set off from Saudárkrókur early, while it was still dark. The snow had stopped, the roads were clear, and the sun rose to reveal a sight of pristine beauty. The following hours I drove through some of the most beautiful landscape I have seen in my life.

It wasn't any one mountain, or any one view. It was a combination of thick newly fallen snow, smooth lakes, dramatic mountain slopes and desolate emptiness, with only the odd, tiny hut showing any sign of habitation.

And the light. During his visit in 1936, W. H. Auden wrote: 'Iceland is the sun colouring the mountains without being anywhere in sight, even sunk beyond the horizon.' It's still true.

The sun in Iceland is always low, but in winter it is

particularly low. It appears above the horizon at about ten o'clock, brushing clouds, water and mountainsides pink. Then it rolls along the horizon before sinking in another glorious inferno of orange and red. As I drove, the sunlight reflected off the clouds in a diffuse pink, even at midday, shifting to yellow, grey and purple as it brought the shape of the towering cloud formations into dramatic relief. Patches of clear sky were light blue and pure. The rivers were pink or a burnished copper, depending on the angle the sun struck them; in shadow they were a ruffled black. Ice shifted colour from white to black, via grey, yellow and brown.

That day the scenery was constantly changing, and I was constantly pulling over to take photographs. As I approached the town of Borgarnes, billowing steam was added to the mix, as the vapour from geothermal pools condensed in the cold air.

It was all glorious.

The weather in Reykjavík is uninspiring. Winters are about the same temperature as Hamburg, but summers don't get as warm. It is milder than you would think in winter: the temperature only dips a few degrees below zero, nothing like the freezes felt in Chicago or Moscow, which are much further south. Trouble is, it doesn't get that warm in summer: temperatures rarely rise above 15 °C – the average high is only 13 °C in July.

The real problem is the wind and the rain. Rain comes in many different forms. When it rains hard, it can feel like someone pouring a bucket of water on your head. Or it can feel like someone throwing a bucket of water at you from the pavement, if it's windy. No umbrella has been known to survive in Iceland: they die rapidly, torn to shreds by the wind. There are two ways of dealing with the wind. One is to face directly into it and lean. The other is to stay inside and read a book.

However, they say that if you don't like the weather in Reykjavík, just wait ten minutes and try again. That wind blows a series of weather fronts in from the Atlantic, where the warm water of the Gulf Stream creates small angry balls of low pressure, which sweep through Iceland, bringing dark clouds, heavy rain, but then crystal-clear skies, puffy clouds and rainbows. Lots of beautiful rainbows, many of them doubles.

They say there is no such thing as bad weather, just bad clothing. I'm not convinced by this. Icelanders mock tourists in Reykjavík for walking around their capital in cagoules or bright ski jackets. Icelanders own stylish dark-coloured coats, waterproof and windproof with warm padding and hoods for walking around the city. I suspect these are expensive. They have another wardrobe of expensive outdoor gear for prancing around the countryside in blizzards. Their fancy city coats would make no sense in Milan or Madrid, or even London or Paris, so I am with the tourists. If Thor, or whoever, is chucking buckets of water down on Reykjavík, then wear your bright orange rain jacket and be damned. Just don't rely on an umbrella to protect you.

Reykjavík is in the south-west corner of Iceland and receives the brunt of the Atlantic weather. To the north, in Akureyri, the weather is slightly better. On the mountains – and much of Iceland is mountainous – the weather is naturally worse: the wind stronger and the temperature lower. Large areas of the highlands in the uninhabited interior of the country lie in rain shadow and don't receive any rainfall at all. They are effectively deserts. Deserts with rivers, as meltwater from glaciers fifty kilometres away rushes through them on the way to the sea.

The higher the latitude, the greater the difference between summer and winter. Iceland is only just below the Arctic Circle, so in midwinter it is dark nearly all the time. Daylight is only a few hours. In practice, dawn turns into dusk at lunchtime. As you can imagine, this has a depressing effect on locals. They go to work in the dark; they come home in the dark. It was even worse in the old days when most Icelanders lived on isolated farms. They essentially stayed indoors all winter, in their living quarters above the animals whose heat kept them warm. They knitted, they read, they milked the cow, they moved hay about. They hibernated.

Because of its proximity to the Arctic Circle, in theory the sun in Iceland is visible for a short period every day, even at midwinter. But that is not true for the town of Ísafjördur, in the West Fjords, which is wedged between high mountains. There they last see the sun on 16 November, and it returns on 25 January. They have *sólarkaffi* – coffee and pancakes – to celebrate on the 25th.

But there are many good things about Iceland in winter. Icelandic houses are nothing much to look at from the outside, but they are cosy on the inside: small, warm, often lit with candles. As I have described, Iceland can look beautiful under snow, especially if the sun manages to peek out between or below the clouds. In my opinion, the best time to visit a hot pot at an outdoor swimming pool or the world-famous Blue Lagoon is in winter, where your body is warm, your nose is cold, and steam billows up from the water, through which you catch glimpses of snow-covered rock. Admittedly, you have to endure the bracing dash over the few short yards from changing room to pool.

Then there are the Northern Lights. This phenomenon is present in winter and summer, but you can only see them when it is dark, so winter is much the better season than summer. And you need clear skies, which in Iceland requires optimism and good luck. The Lights, also known as the aurora borealis, are the result of solar wind disturbing the magnetosphere and altering the trajectories of charged particles in the upper atmosphere, causing them to emit light.

The Northern Lights come in many different forms: at their weakest they are thin trails of white; at their strongest they take the form of shimmering curtains of green, yellow and red, which drape the whole night sky. They don't perform every night – their strength varies. It's not the case that they are strongest near the North Pole; in fact there is a band that surrounds the earth close to the Arctic Circle where they are at maximum strength, and the centre of this band passes right over Iceland, which suggests the country is a good place to see them. If it isn't cloudy.

There have been magnificent pictures taken of the Northern Lights, but not by me. You need to be clever with a camera. Yet no camera can do the aurora justice. You need to be standing underneath the black of the night sky stretching from horizon to horizon all around you. Then the lights play, shifting, shimmering, disappearing and reappearing, first in one part of the sky and then another. It's all about swivelling your neck and dropping your jaw.

There are a number of festivals to relieve the tedium of the long night-days. Christmas is as big a deal in Iceland as everywhere else. The mischievous 'Yule lads' come in the days before Christmas to place gifts in children's shoes. Like much of Northern Europe, Christmas Eve is more important than Christmas Day. There is a tradition of everyone giving each other books; I thoroughly approve of this. Carols are sung, board games are played, the Christmas tree glimmers. A traditional Christmas Eve dinner might be thick rice soup mixed with cinnamon and sugar, dark ptarmigan with red cabbage, and frothy pineapple mousse. There is a lot of *hangikjöt* around at this time of year, delicious smoked lamb.

Then, a few days later, comes New Year's Eve. The entire nation watches a satirical comedy show on TV, and then emerges to launch their elaborate arsenals of fireworks at each other. In January or February, the Icelanders celebrate *thorrablót*, a feast of all the traditional foods: putrefied shark, ram's testicles, congealed sheep's blood wrapped in a ram's stomach and boiled sheep's head, all washed down with 'black death'. Yum yum. Eventually, Icelanders display their elevated sense of irony with 'the first day of summer', which takes place in a snowstorm some time in April.

Nordic countries are often depicted as being dark, gloomy and depressing. But that is only half the story. The other half is summer, when the sun shines for twenty-one hours. It is light at 11 p.m. in Reykjavík on a Saturday night when the crowds are going into the bars and it is light at 2 a.m. when they are leaving. It is an extraordinary sight to see so many drunk people so early in the morning.

Icelanders become manic. Their eyes sparkle bright blue, but there are red rims around them. On the farms, if winter was the time of snoozing, summer was the time of eighteen-hour days. A whole year's farming had to be crammed into a few short months. In particular the hay had to be harvested to feed the livestock over the winter. Today Icelanders are still busy eighteen hours a day in summer. Eight o'clock in the evening feels like mid-afternoon. It can be difficult trying to go to sleep at ten thirty when your body is telling you it is early evening.

Despite the lack of trees, there are autumn colours in Iceland. Various berries and dwarf willows and birches change colour, and the lava fields and heathlands glow in purples and oranges. It's also the time of the *réttir*, the annual round-up, when the members of a farming community get on their horses and spend three days scouring the mountains with their sheepdogs rounding up their sheep. The beasts are brought down to pens, sorted by the farmers, and put in barns for the winter. The farmers and their children get very excited at seeing their sheep again, who all have their own names, and a good time is had by all. I have no idea what the sheep think about it. I wrote a short story called *The Super Recogniser of Vík* about a farmer who was expert at recognizing sheep and was dragged to Reykjavík by Magnus to look at CCTV to find a burglar.

So when is the best time to come to Iceland? Most people come in July and August: these are the two warmest months, and of course children are on school holiday. Personally, I avoid these two months. I'd rather spend the summer months somewhere where the temperature exceeds 20 °C. More importantly, Iceland is crowded. Tourist numbers are rocketing: from only a few hundred thousand at the time of the *kreppa* to over two million a year now. Despite a construction frenzy in Reykjavík, the infrastructure can't keep up. It's hard for locals to rent accommodation in Reykjavík because most apartments coming on the market are rented out on Airbnb. More worryingly, there are not enough public toilets, especially out in the countryside. This infrastructure is at its most overstretched in July and August.

The Icelandic landscape is much more delicate than it looks; hordes of tourists' walking boots can wreak havoc on moss and lichens trying to establish themselves on new lava. The paradox of travelling a thousand miles to a desolate spot to enjoy the isolation is highlighted when dozens of others are doing it too. Summer is also the time when volunteer search-and-rescue teams become fed up with rescuing tourists who have wandered into the wrong place at the wrong time.

I see I have mentioned the idiotic acts of tourists a number of times in this book. It's not that all tourists are stupid – clearly most are not – but the moronic minority gives the rest of us a bad reputation with the locals.

So I would visit in the slightly quieter months of May and June, or September to November. In September the grass is still green, the snow has yet to fall and it's beginning to be possible to see the Northern Lights. In November, you can experience winter and yet still enjoy a little daylight. Go expecting bad weather; that way you won't be disappointed.

18   GREENLAND AND VINLAND

I first heard of Gudrídur Thorbjarnardóttir, or Gudrid the Wanderer, when I was visiting my ecclesiastical contact, the Reverend Sara. She showed me her church, an amazing modern building with an altar bathed in light reflected off water, in the Reykjavík suburb of Grafarholt. The church was dedicated to Gudrid. She told me about Gudrid's travels from Iceland to North America and back again, and then on to Rome. I found this extraordinary; I still do.

As I discovered more about Gudrid, I determined to write a book about her. But writing a twenty-first-century detective novel about a Viking explorer is not easy. It took me several years to alight on a way of doing it, but I got there in the end. A TV crew is making a documentary about Gudrid, following in her footsteps to Greenland and North America, when someone is murdered. Magnus investigates.

Before Magnus could get on the case, I needed to do my own investigation. There are two sagas which give a broad picture of the Viking settlement of Greenland and exploration of North America: *The Saga of the*

Greenlanders, and *The Saga of Erik the Red*, together known as *The Vinland Sagas*, and published as such by Penguin Classics. These describe the following story. The outlaw Erik the Red sailed from Iceland and established himself at a farm at Brattahlíd in the south-west of Greenland. Gudrid followed him, with her first husband, who died soon after they arrived in Greenland. Vikings settled along the west coast of Greenland, at the 'Eastern Settlement' around what is now Qaqortoq, and the 'Western Settlement' further up the coast near what is now the capital, Nuuk.

The two sagas disagree on who first made landfall in North America, which became known as 'Vinland'. One saga says it was Bjarni Herjólfsson, who got lost on the way to Greenland, the other says it was Leif Eriksson, Erik the Red's son. These days Leif seems to get all the credit. Anyway, Leif, Thorfinn Karlsefni and Thorfinn's new wife Gudrid made a series of expeditions to Vinland, or Vínland in Old Norse, so called because of the discovery of grapes there. The sagas describe the establishment of temporary settlements at 'Leif's Booths' and 'Keel Point', as well as a tantalizing journey far to the south to a place called 'Hop', which is described in some detail.

The Norse remained in Greenland until the fifteenth century. Around the year 1000, Northern Europe was relatively warm, and it was possible to grow crops in Greenland. Greenlanders traded with Iceland and England, narwhal horns being a particularly profitable export, as we have seen. Most of Greenland is covered with a massive block of ice, many miles deep, but there are small patches of lush green around the south coast. One of these is Brattahlíd, now known as Qassiarsuk, which is on the opposite side of the fjord from the former US airbase and now international airport at Narsarsuaq. You can still see the remains of Erik the Red's farm, and a replica stands a couple of hundred metres away. In July, the ruins are knee-deep in lush green grass and wild flowers; white and blue icebergs drift sedately by in the fjord. Sheep farming was reintroduced to the area in the 1920s.

The mystery about Greenland isn't how it was settled but how it was abandoned. As the thirteenth century progressed, the climate became colder. The southern fjords were iced up for much of the year. Greenland had been uninhabited when the Norsemen arrived, but in the twelfth century the Inuit appeared. It's not clear whether they and the Norsemen fought, but the Inuit were expert hunters, and it is probable that they outcompeted the Norsemen, especially when it became too cold for the Viking farmers to grow crops.

The last recorded mention of the Greenland settlement is the description of a wedding at Hvalsey in 1409 by a visiting merchant from Iceland – the ruins of the Norse church there still stand. Eventually the harbours of Greenland were frozen all the year round. It's not clear what happened to the surviving settlers: some speculate that they headed south to Vinland, some think they were overwhelmed by the Inuit, and others believe they starved to death in the cold. I shiver just to think about those last settlers trapped year round by sea ice, waiting for ships from the outside world that never came.

There is much less archaeological evidence for a Viking presence in North America; indeed, until 1961 there was none. Despite the compelling descriptions in the sagas, many historians preferred to write them off as myth, ensuring that the credit for discovering America lay with the Genoese Christopher Columbus. However, in 1961 a Norwegian couple, Anne and Helge Ingstad, discovered evidence of a Norse settlement at L'Anse aux Meadows in Newfoundland. Since then various other Viking artefacts have been found in Canada, especially to the north on Baffin Island and Ellesmere Island.

There remains the question of how far Thorfinn Karlsefni and Gudrid travelled south, in other words where this mysterious place Hop is. The Vikings stayed there for a couple of summers, before being driven out by the locals, or 'Skraelings' as the Norse called them. There are clues about grapes, self-sown wheat, a river running north to south, and a lagoon right by the sea (*hóp* means 'tidal lagoon'). Candidate locations include the St Lawrence estuary, Buzzard's Bay near Cape Cod, Narragansett in Rhode Island and even Brooklyn. The truth is we don't know. That's the kind of gap in the historical record I love. It's crying out for a novel to fill it.

A quantity of spurious Viking remains have been found in the United States. Most are clearly fakes. One of the most famous is the Kensington rune stone – Kensington is a small town in Minnesota – which was discovered by a Swedish farmer in 1898. This bore an inscription in runes saying the equivalent of '30 Vikings woz here 1362'. This seems an obvious fake – Minnesota is a long way from the Atlantic. But much to my surprise, having read the evidence, I suspect that the stone may indeed be genuine, and that a Viking party travelled down from the Hudson Bay or along the Great Lakes water system to Minnesota. It is extraordinary how far Viking trading routes stretched: from Byzantium in the east, through Russia and the Baltic to Iceland and then on to Greenland and Vinland. We shouldn't underestimate the Norsemen's ability to cover large distances by sea, river and lake.

Oscar Wilde is supposed to have said: 'The Icelanders

are the most intelligent race on earth, because they discovered America and never told anyone.' Much of the scepticism of historians towards the idea that Icelanders discovered America comes from Italians or Italian Americans who are big fans of Columbus. They have a particular problem with a visit Columbus may or may not have made to Iceland in 1477, fifteen years before he set sail on the *Santa María*. The journey was reported by Columbus himself in his letter to Queen Isabella many years later, but he was frustratingly vague, talking about a land called 'Thile' and tides of extraordinary variation. But his account agrees with the stories of an Italian nobleman staying near Ólafsvík.

The claims by some historians that if Columbus did visit Iceland he would have been unlikely to hear of Vinland are laughable. I quote from an article in a learned historical journal I read in the British Library:

> There is no need to suggest that he [Columbus] learned of the medieval Greenland colony: Icelanders had lost interest in it after Norway took control of contacts with it . . . He is still less likely to have heard of the Vinland sagas, even if they had been retained in folk memory, which is very doubtful, or had been written down in unintelligible language between the twelfth and fourteenth centuries.

This is one of the all-time classic underestimations of Iceland. The fifteenth century was the greatest period when the sagas were copied. Iceland was full of priests who understood Latin. Icelanders had traded with Greenland in living memory; some had attended a wedding there seventy years before. If Columbus did visit Iceland in 1477, as he claimed he did, he would most certainly have heard about Vinland.

Plenty to get my teeth into. In September 2018, almost ten years after I had first heard of Gudrid and visited Ingjaldshóll where Columbus is rumoured to have stayed, *The Wanderer* was published.

19 COVID-19

I can't remember when I first heard about the virus named after a Mexican beer that was running rampant in some city in China which I definitely hadn't heard of. Some time in January 2020, I suspect. I know we had a holiday to India booked, leaving on 27 March, and my wife and I discussed whether we should pay the balance due, or abandon our deposit. Would the virus spread to India by then? Probably not.

The twenty-seventh of March is my wife's birthday, and we celebrated it not on a flight to Delhi, but in double lockdown in our flat in London. Not only were we suffering the general restrictions that the government had imposed on Britain, but our son was recovering from COVID himself, and we were self-isolating.

The virus is no joke. It has caused serious difficulties for most of the world's population, including loss of liberty, loss of family contact, loss of employment and, for far too many, loss of life. I was relatively unscathed. My working day before the pandemic mostly consisted of sitting at my desk tapping into my computer. It still does.

I finished the first draft of my stand-alone thriller *The Diplomat's Wife* in May, and decided that my next would be a Magnus crime novel. As I began to think about this, two problems arose.

The first was one that must have faced all novelists during 2020. How should I treat the virus? Should I set the book in pre-virus 2019? Should I come up with a plot centred on COVID? Should I acknowledge COVID going about its evil work in the background? Or should I set the novel in some kind of alternative world untouched by masks, lockdowns and quarantine?

I asked my readers. I send occasional emails to a few thousand of them, and I asked what they would like to read. The result was interesting. A large majority, perhaps 80 per cent, wanted to see COVID in the next Magnus book, split between those who thought it should have its own plot and those who preferred a background role. A minority disagreed, but boy did they disagree strongly. They were fed up to the back teeth with the virus, and the last thing they wanted to do was read about it.

I tended to agree with the latter camp. During lockdown, I had enjoyed losing myself in pre-war Berlin and Paris, the setting for *The Diplomat's Wife*, and I really didn't want to spend a year fussing about COVID in my book as well as in real life. On the other hand, as you can tell by now, I do like to get things right, and so I couldn't bring myself to ignore the virus completely. So I decided to acknowledge it, but give it a background role.

The second problem was how to research the damned disease. For starters, it's a moving target. Life changes month by month with its ebb and flow. I decided to travel to Iceland sometime in the following twelve months, and place most of the action in the novel in whatever month my trip turned out to be. My best guess was that I would go to the crime festival Iceland Noir in November, and take a couple of extra days to observe and document daily life in Iceland at that time.

Iceland's response to the coronavirus confirmed many of the traits that we have discussed in the book so far. They were quick, and they showed plenty of initiative. As soon as they heard about the epidemic in Wuhan in January, public health officials got together and drew up a plan. This involved the standard public health reaction – preparing protective equipment, alerting hospitals, and setting up a contact tracing system. Interestingly, from my point of view, the contact tracing team was led by a police detective and comprised two more policemen, a criminologist and two nurses. I have no doubt that either Magnus or Vigdís were on this team.

The response of Kári Stefánsson, the CEO of DeCode, Iceland's largest biotech company, which specializes in genetic sequencing, was typical. He heard a piece on the lethality of the virus on the radio driving into work and immediately decided that his firm would do all it could to help. He made himself a real pain to the prime minister and everyone else, but Iceland very swiftly had the kind of testing system in place that bigger countries – the United Kingdom, for example – would be unable to replicate after many months.

This worked fine for a few weeks, but then Iceland ran into one of the other traits mentioned in this book: Icelanders don't really like doing what they are told. They are independent people. So quite a few broke the rules, and for a few weeks the disease ran rampant. Once again, Iceland found itself briefly on top of global per capita league tables, this time for coronavirus infections. But then another trait kicked in: trust. A triumvirate of three officials – the director of emergency management, the chief epidemiologist and the director of health – gave briefings at 2 p.m. every day unencumbered by politicians.

The people believed them. This wasn't just a set of petty rules, this was a natural disaster, comparable to a volcanic eruption or a blizzard. The Icelanders pulled together. They followed the rules.

By May, cases were right down to only two in a week. Life became almost normal. People went to restaurants and bars, no one wore a mask, the disease seemed to be conquered.

But there were consequences. As we have seen, Iceland's biggest industry had become tourism. There were no foreign tourists. None. Economic disaster loomed for all those in the tourist trade, from the baristas in the cafés to the puffin-shop workers to the barmen and chambermaids in hotels. And, of course, the businessmen and -women who owned these places.

So they came up with a plan, which sounded quite clever to me. In July they allowed foreigners to come to Iceland again, provided they either spent two weeks in quarantine or paid for a COVID test. A dribble of tourists arrived that month.

The plan suffered a swift setback when two Romanians were arrested having broken into a shop in Selfoss. It turned out that not only had they skipped quarantine, but they were positive for the disease. A manhunt was launched for three of their companions who were loose somewhere in the country, a manhunt that was hampered because a large proportion of the police force of South Iceland had been involved in the arrests, and had to go into quarantine themselves.

This proved to be a one-off incident, but with the tourists came the disease. Slowly at first. There was a brief little scandal when two quarantined England footballers lured a couple of local women back to their hotel.

Then the Frenchmen came. It only took two of them. They were supposed to be in quarantine but they didn't understand the instructions, so they went to a pub called the Irishman, and then a restaurant, Brewdog. Within a week there were a hundred cases in Reykjavík related to those two venues. The virus was loose in Iceland again. Restrictions were imposed on the locals and on foreign tourists. The streets of Reykjavík became empty, and the beds in the National Hospital began to fill. DeCode's analysis of the virus then present in Iceland showed that it was a strain from France.

Iceland Noir was cancelled and with it my planned trip to Iceland in November. Given the tougher quarantining restrictions in Iceland, and in England for that matter, I am not sure when I will be able to go. When you are writing about Iceland, the season matters: Reykjavík in February is very different from Reykjavík in May. I need to make some decision on this before I start writing.

A moving target.

EPILOGUE

Plan C worked.

Where the Shadows Lie was published in Britain and America, and in fourteen other languages, including Icelandic. I travelled to Iceland for a book tour to publicize the novel, which is entitled *Hringnum Lokad*. After a couple of days chatting to a bewildering number of journalists, I found myself on the Icelandic talk show *Silfur Egils*, in front of the man himself, Egill Helgason, the scourge of corrupt politicians and economy-wrecking bankers. And perhaps of presumptuous foreign writers, guests with unclear eyes.

I was a little scared. I told myself no one I knew would see the programme, just a bunch of Icelanders, and who cared about them? Then it came to me. I did. I cared very much.

The first question the fearsome Egill asked me was: 'How do you manage to write so accurately about Iceland? Is it true that your mother was born here?' This question made me smile with pride: suddenly I wished that the whole world spoke Icelandic and tuned into *Silfur Egils*. I also smiled at the evidence of the energetic Icelandic rumour mill going off at half-cock; I explained to Egill that my mother was born in Hampstead.

Since then, I have written four more novels featuring Magnus, and a couple of sixty-page novellas. I have revisited Iceland many times, and I have grown to love it, despite the appalling weather.

Having read this book, I hope you can see why.

APPENDIX: SOURCES

Here is a more detailed list of the various sources I have used to find out about Iceland over the last few years. I have listed them in rough order of usefulness and enjoyment. I have also included sub-sections entitled 'From the Reading Pile', which are those books I haven't got to yet, but seem worth a look.

This list is far from comprehensive. Its obvious weakness is that it only lists books published in English, thereby omitting all kinds of books only available in Icelandic, as well as books about Iceland in German, French, Spanish and other languages. And I haven't included every book I have read on the subject: *Archaeological Excavations at Qassiarsuk 2005–2006* didn't make the cut, for example.

So, here goes:

Books
Non-Fiction
***Icelandic Saga* by Magnus Magnusson**

A trip around Iceland, beautifully combining its landscape and its history.

The Little Book of the Icelanders by **Alda Sigmundsdóttir**

A little book about Iceland and its quirks by an Icelandic-Canadian writer with a keen eye. Alda's other 'Little Books' include *Iceland in the Old Days, Tourists in Iceland* and *The Icelandic Language.*

Dreaming of Iceland by **Sally Magnusson**

A wonderful tale of a week-long trip around Iceland by Sally Magnusson and her father Magnus.

Ring of Seasons by **Terry Lacy**

An affectionate description of Iceland by an American who lives there.

Names for the Sea: Strangers in Iceland by **Sarah Moss**

A beautifully written account of an English novelist and academic's year at the University of Iceland during the financial crash and the eruption of Eyjafjallajökull. It wasn't all easy.

Waking Up in Iceland by **Paul Sullivan**

An account of following the music scene in Reykjavík by a perceptive music journalist.

The Rough Guide to Iceland by **David Leffman and James Proctor**

Lonely Planet Iceland by Fran Parnell and Brandon Presser

Never underestimate the usefulness of well-written and carefully researched travel guides, of which these two are good examples.

Across Iceland by Olive Murray Chapman

An intrepid Scottish woman's account of her travels across Iceland in 1930, describing the warm welcome she received and the primitive living standards of the time. This lady was a lot tougher than Messrs Auden and MacNeice (see below).

Meltdown Iceland by Roger Boyes

A clear account of the *kreppa*, the financial crash that swept through Iceland in 2008–2010, by a foreign correspondent from *The Times*.

Frozen Assets by Ármann Thorvaldsson

Another account of the *kreppa*, this time from one of the bankers who helped bring it about.

Icelandic Folk Legends translated by Alda Sigmundsdóttir
Icelandic Folk and Fairy Tales translated by May and Hallberg Hallmundsson

Good translations of Iceland's wonderful folk tales featuring trolls, elves, hidden people, ghosts, ravens, sea monsters and a polar bear. Best dipped in and out of rather than read all in one sitting, in my opinion.

A Traveller's Guide to Icelandic Folk Tales by Jón R. Hjálmarsson

A fascinating book of sixty folk tales from different locations around Iceland, each story including a description of the countryside where it took place. Good to pack for an Icelandic road trip.

Poetry
Letters from Iceland by W. H. Auden and Louis MacNeice

School reports in poetry and prose from two poets sent on a boondoggle to Iceland in the 1930s by their publisher, Faber.

Moon Country by Simon Armitage and Glyn Maxwell

A follow-up pilgrimage to Iceland made by two leading British poets, once again paid for by Faber.

Fiction (Non-Crime) in Icelandic
Independent People by Halldór Laxness (tr. J. A. Thompson)

The great Icelandic novel.

Under the Glacier by Halldór Laxness (tr. Magnus Magnusson)

An emissary from the Bishop of Iceland arrives in an eccentric community under the Snaefells glacier.

101 Reykjavík by Hallgrímur Helgason (tr. Brian Fitzgibbon)

A sardonic look at the life of a thirty-year-old slacker in

Reykjavík who still lives with his mum. Great depiction of Reykjavík at night; I have yet to meet a slacker there, though.

The Thief of Time by Steinunn Sigurdardóttir (tr. Rory McTurk)

The story of a love affair, which touches intriguingly on class, a phenomenon that lurks only half visible in Icelandic society. One of three Sigurdardóttirs on this list: they are not sisters.

The Blue Fox by Sjón (tr. Victoria Cribb)

A charming story by Iceland's leading contemporary literary author and poet about the hunt for an elusive blue fox. Applies magical realism successfully to the Icelandic landscape.

From the Reading Pile:

Heida: A Shepherd at the Edge of the World by Heida Asgeirsdóttir and Steinunn Sigurdardóttir (tr. Philip Roughton)

The memoir of an international model turned lonely sheep farmer.

Fiction (Non-Crime) in English

The Killer's Guide to Iceland by Zane Radcliffe

An underrated novel about an Englishman's visit to his girlfriend in Iceland, which goes badly wrong. Imaginative descriptions of the country and its people and a good story. Should be in the crime section, really.

The Sea Road by Margaret Elphinstone

A retelling of the life of Gudrid the Wanderer, with the gaps left by the sagas filled in.

The Sealwoman's Gift by Sally Magnusson

The story of an Icelandic woman kidnapped by Barbary pirates in the seventeenth century and taken to North Africa. Bewitching.

Running Blind by Desmond Bagley

Classic 1960s spy caper involving a British agent with a mysterious package being chased all the way around Iceland, literally circumnavigating the island. Much loved by many.

From the Reading Pile:

Burial Rites by Hannah Kent

An acclaimed novel about an Icelandic woman sentenced to death in 1829.

<u>Sagas</u>

See Chapter Nine. These are the ones I enjoy the most. It is well worth paying for a good translation – here the Penguin Classics brand earns its reputation for reliability. Penguin publishes a 700-page compendium of about thirty of them, entitled *The Sagas of the Icelanders*.

Njal's Saga

The longest and best. A legal thriller. The hero is Njál, a canny lawyer who tries and fails to mediate between families bearing grudges.

Egil's Saga

Egil was a great warrior with a bad temper and a flair for poetry.

The Laxdaela Saga

A love triangle between three inhabitants of Breidafjördur: Gudrun, Kjartan and Bolli. Much blood is shed. Gudrun is one of the most fascinating characters in the sagas.

Grettir's Saga

Grettir is an outlaw with a bad temper who fights humans and the undead.

Eyrbyggja Saga or *The Saga of the People of Eyri*

The quarrels of various families in Snaefellsnes with a few berserkers, ghosts and soothsayers thrown in.

The Saga of the Volsungs

The story of the ring. It's been around for a while (both the ring *and* its story).

The Saga of Erik the Red
The Greenlanders' Saga

The travels of Erik and other Norsemen to Iceland, then Greenland and North America. (See Chapter Eighteen.)

Fiction – Crime

When I first started researching Iceland, only one crime writer was regularly published in English, Arnaldur Indridason. At about the time my first novel set in Iceland was published, so was Yrsa Sigurdardóttir's first novel translated into English, *Last Rituals*. For many years Yrsa and Arnaldur fought toe-to-toe for top slot in the all-important Icelandic Christmas bestseller list.

On one of my early trips to Iceland, I had dinner with my publisher Pétur at an old restaurant by the Tjörnin in Reykjavík. He introduced me to two of his authors, Lilja Sigurdardóttir and Ragnar Jónasson. He assured me both were very good, but neither was published in English. Well, they are now, to justified worldwide acclaim.

Lastly, I should mention Quentin Bates, a fellow Englishman whose first crime novel set in Iceland came out at the same time as *Where the Shadows Lie*. As well as writing his own novels, Quentin translated extracts of Lilja and Ragnar's books into English to help them find a publisher, and then, when they succeeded, translated the entire novels.

In other words, this list is not unbiased. This book is dedicated to four of the authors on the list. I like them and I love their books. And they all tell you a lot about life in Iceland. My only regret is that for several years I avoided reading them, for fear of clouding my own plot ideas.

Arnaldur Indridason

Arnaldur's detective, Erlendur, is a policeman of the old school. He yearns for the farm of his childhood in the east of Iceland and he enjoys a sheep's head for lunch. Arnaldur's books examine the conflict between the old and the new in Iceland's society, as well as solving some fascinating crimes. *Silence of the Grave*, about the discovery of bones dating from the Second World War, won the British Crime Writers' Association Gold Dagger in 2005. I'm not sure whether that is my favourite or *Tainted Blood*, also known as *Jar City*, a novel about genetic research, which was made into a film.

Yrsa Sigurdardóttir

Yrsa's first crime novel translated into English was *Last Rituals*, featuring a young, disorganized lawyer, Thóra. She followed up with several more Thóra books, and then another series featuring the child psychologist, Freyja, as well as a few suspense novels. Yrsa is not afraid of ghosts, or at least writing about them. *I Remember You* is deeply unsettling. I think my favourite is *The Legacy*, one of the Freyja series.

Quentin Bates

Quentin's detective is Gunnhildur, a no-nonsense detective with a complicated family. Although British like me, Quentin knows much more than me about Iceland: his wife is Icelandic and he spent many years working on Icelandic trawlers. He depicts the chaos of Icelandic life: the messy family structures of half-brothers and stepsisters and he is good on the criminals, especially of the hapless variety.

Ragnar Jónasson

Ragnar was obsessed with Agatha Christie as a child, and started translating her novels into Icelandic at the age of nineteen. His first series featured the naive detective Ari Thór. His more recent series is about Hulda, a detective coming up to retirement, and is very popular in Germany.

Lilja Sigurdardóttir

Lilja has written three novels about Sonja, a desperate

single mother driven to drug smuggling: *Snare*, *Trap* and *Cage*, and a political thriller, *Betrayal*. Sonja's problems include her lesbian love life, her bankster ex-husband and assorted unpleasant types. Original and absorbing, Lilja's books have won worldwide acclaim. The French, in particular, seem to like them.

Viktor Arnar Ingólfsson

Viktor Arnar's *The Flatey Enigma* is set in 1960 on the tiny island of Flatey, home of the famous saga collection the *Flateyjarbók*. It's a murder mystery with a literary puzzle included. A different flavour from the other crime novels in this list. His day job is to write the traffic signs in Iceland.

Other Icelandic crime writers translated into English include **Aevar Örn Jósepsson**, **Árni Thórarinsson**, **Eva Björg Aegisdóttir** and **Sólveig Pálsdóttir**. There are more to come, including one by a very nice chap called Óskar.

There is a rumour that Icelandic Prime Minister **Katrín Jakobsdóttir** is planning to write a crime novel, with some help from Ragnar. She has a PhD in crime fiction; I've heard her talk on the subject, and she really knows her stuff, as does Ragnar obviously, so the book may turn out to be pretty good.

Film and TV

Several of these are adaptations of the books above.

Trapped

A TV detective series created by Iceland's foremost

director, Baltasar Kormákur. It is set in a village in the East Fjords, cut off by snow. A body is found, the weekly ferry from Denmark is suspected, and the burly local police chief Andri investigates. Very good.

The Valhalla Murders

A classic police detective TV series. A succession of murders are linked to a children's home – Valhalla. Kata must solve the crimes, with the help of an enigmatic Icelandic expat just back from Oslo. Beautiful images of Reykjavík in the snow and really quite a lot of blood.

Woman at War

My favourite Icelandic film. A choir conductor named Halla is an eco-terrorist, destroying power lines supplying an aluminium plant, all the time watched by three musicians who provide the score. Her plan to adopt a child from the Ukraine gets in the way of things. Quirky, in the best Icelandic manner.

101 Reykjavík

A film of the book about Hlynur, the slacker who lives with his mum.

Rams

A beautiful film about two neighbouring sheep farmers in a remote dale who hate each other and haven't spoken for decades.

The Night Shift

A comedy set in a petrol station at night. Jón Gnarr, who became mayor of Reykjavík, is the night manager. An

Icelandic version of *The Office*, it built up a cult following in the UK.

I Remember You

A deeply unsettling film about a group of visitors to a remote island who stumble across evidence of a missing child. Scary. Based on Yrsa's book.

Pressa

A TV series about tabloid journalists. All the ethical and professional conflicts you would expect, in an Icelandic setting. I enjoyed it.

Jar City

A film of the book by Arnaldur Indridason. A classic detective story with a biotech twist. Ingvar Eggert Sigurdsson makes an excellent Erlendur (he gets demoted to be the sergeant sidekick in *Trapped*, above).

Nói Albinói

A film of teenage anomie set in an isolated Icelandic town in the middle of winter, filmed in Bolungarvík. It's a little bleak. Very bleak. But memorable.

The Seagull's Laughter

Set in an Icelandic fishing village in the 1950s, it tells the story of a local girl made good in America returning to her home town.

Cold Fever

Distinctly   weird   Icelandic-Japanese   film   about   a

Japanese man lost in Iceland in winter. At one point he is saved by an elf. I enjoyed it, I'm not quite sure why.

To Be Watched:

The Deep

The story of a man who was shipwrecked and survived. With the big guy from *Trapped*.

Magazines and Newspapers

Iceland Review

A beautifully produced quarterly magazine that has been going for decades. Its journalists are often articulate English-speaking foreigners who love Iceland such as Eliza Reid, a Canadian whose husband is now president. Outstanding photographs. Worth becoming a subscriber: it costs about 60 euros a year, and it keeps you in touch with Iceland.

The Reykjavík Grapevine

An always interesting English-language newspaper. Irreverent, but relevant. Good for what's on where.

The Internet

There are a wealth of blogs about Iceland that come and go. Some are very good. Reading through this book, I realize that my two most important sources for interesting information about Iceland are blogs by Alda and Yrsa. Also, both the *Iceland Review* and *The Reykjavík Grapevine* have a strong internet presence.

A note of warning: the *Iceland Review*, the *Reykjavík Grapevine* and Alda's blogs and pages reflect a left-of-centre opinion. This is shared by many Icelanders, but not all of them: the right-wing Independent Party often wins elections. I sometimes need to remind myself that even if these three sources agree on an issue, especially a political one, they are not speaking for all Icelanders.

Alda Sigmundsdóttir

Alda is an Icelander who was brought up in Canada and as such is well placed to explain her country to foreigners. She used to work as a journalist for the *Iceland Review*, writing a weather report which digressed. This became a lively and informative blog: the *Iceland Weather Report*. She has stopped writing this now, but she has an occasional blog, an email newsletter, a Facebook page and a Twitter account which are worth following. Go to aldasigmunds.com for more information. She has also written a number of 'Little Books' (see above), and a novel, *Unraveled*.

Yrsa Sigurdardóttir

Yrsa used to write a witty and perceptive blog for Murder Is Everywhere, which included some great stories about Iceland. Those articles are still on their site somewhere, but they are difficult to track down. You can try rummaging on the site www.murderiseverywhere. blogspot.com.

ACKNOWLEDGMENTS

I would like to thank the numerous people mentioned in this book who have helped me learn about Iceland over the years. Thanks are due in particular to Bragi Thór Valsson for his patient help in checking the manuscript and saving me from some embarrassing errors. And Richenda Todd and Liz Hatherell, who applied to this book the skills they have picked up in editing my various Magnus novels. Thanks also to Jeff Edwards who drew the map. But if there was ever a book where the errors belong to the author, it's this one.

FREE BOOK

A Message from Michael Ridpath
  Get a Free 60-page story

If you would like to try one of my stories about Magnus for free, then sign up to my mailing list. I will send you a free copy of THE POLAR BEAR KILLING, a 60-page story set in north-east Iceland.

A starving polar bear swims ashore in a remote Icelandic village and is shot by the local policeman. Two days later, the policeman is found dead on a hill above the village. A polar bear justice novella with an Icelandic twist.

To sign up to the mailing list and get your free copy of THE POLAR BEAR KILLING, go to my website www. michaelridpath.com and click on the link for "Free Download" of *The Polar Bear Killing*.

For more information on my other Magnus books, please read on...

ALSO BY MICHAEL RIDPATH

Where the Shadows Lie

One thousand years ago: An Icelandic warrior returns from battle, bearing a ring cut from the right hand of his foe.

Seventy years ago: An Oxford professor, working from a secret source, creates the twentieth century's most pervasive legend. The professor's name? John Ronald Reuel Tolkien.

Six hours ago: An expert on Old Norse literature, Agnar Haraldsson, is murdered.

Everything is connected, but to discover how, Detective Magnus Jonson must venture where the shadows lie...

66° North (Far North in the US)

Iceland 1934: Two boys playing in the lava fields that surround their isolated farmsteads see something they shouldn't have. The consequences will haunt them and their families for generations.

Iceland 2009: the credit crunch bites. The currency has been devalued, savings annihilated, lives ruined. Revolution is in the air, as is the feeling that someone ought to pay the blood price... And in a country with a population of just 300,000 souls, where everyone knows everybody, it isn't hard to draw up a list of those responsible.

And then, one-by-one, to cross them off.

Iceland 2010: As bankers and politicians start to die at home and abroad, it is up to Magnus Jonson to unravel the web of conspirators before they strike again.

But while Magnus investigates the crimes of the present, the crimes of the past are catching up with him.

Meltwater

Iceland, 2010: A group of internet activists have found evidence of a military atrocity in the Middle East. As they prepare to unleash the damning video to the world's media, to the backdrop of the erupting volcano Eyjafjallajökull, one is brutally murdered.

As Magnus Jonson begins to investigate, the list of suspects grows ever longer. From the Chinese government, Israeli military, Italian politicians, even to American College Fraternities, the group has made many enemies. And more are coming to the surface every day...

And with the return of Magnus's brother Ollie to Iceland, the feud that has haunted their family for three generations is about to reignite.

Sea of Stone

Iceland, 2010: Called to investigate a suspected homicide in a remote farmstead, Constable Páll is surprised to find that Sergeant Magnus Jonson is already at the scene. The victim? Magnus's estranged grandfather.

But it quickly becomes apparent that the crime scene has been tampered with, and that Magnus's version of events doesn't add up. Before long, Magnus is arrested for the murder of his grandfather. When it emerges that his younger brother, Ollie, is in Iceland after two decades in America, Páll begins to think that Magnus may not be the only family member in the frame for murder...

The Wanderer

When a young Italian tourist is found brutally murdered at a sacred church in northern Iceland, Magnus Jonson, newly returned to the Reykjavik police force, is called to investigate. At the scene he finds a stunned TV crew, there to film a documentary on the life of the legendary Viking, Gudrid the Wanderer.

Magnus quickly begins to suspect that there may be more links to the murdered woman than anyone in the film crew will acknowledge. As jealousies come to the surface, new tensions replace old friendships, and history begins to rewrite itself, a shocking second murder leads Magnus to question everything he thought he knew.

REVIEW THIS BOOK

I would be really grateful if you could take a moment to review this book. Reviews, even of only a few words, are really important for the success of a book these days.

Thank you.

Michael

CPSIA information can be obtained
at www.ICGtesting.com
Printed in the USA
LVHW020113230621
690927LV00006B/487